SpringerBriefs in Economics

More information about this series at http://www.springer.com/series/8876

Bennie Linde

The Value of Wellness in the Workplace

A Perspective of the Employee-Organisation Relationship in the South African Labour Market

Springer

Bennie Linde
North-West University
Potchefstroom
South Africa

ISSN 2191-5504 ISSN 2191-5512 (electronic)
SpringerBriefs in Economics
ISBN 978-981-287-401-6 ISBN 978-981-287-402-3 (eBook)
DOI 10.1007/978-981-287-402-3

Library of Congress Control Number: 2015930004

Springer Singapore Heidelberg New York Dordrecht London

Printed on acid-free paper

Springer Science+Business Media Singapore Pte Ltd. is part of Springer Science+Business Media (www.springer.com)

Contents

Chapter 1
Work Wellness in South Africa: A History of Change

1.1 Introduction

The wider society is structured by a dynamic and complicated series of systems—for instance the ecological, sociocultural, economical, political, legal, religious, educational and labour relations systems (Bendix 2010; Craig 1975; Finnemore and Van Rensburg 2000; Sztompka 1991). While each of these systems is autonomous, they do not function in isolation (Dunlop 1993). Output generated from one system can become an input for another system, which develops new output that are once again submitted as input into systems in the wider society (Bendix 2010). These systems are in constant change and occasionally subject to transformation and reform (Fink 2001). Toeffler (1999, p. 28) states that "you have to decide whether you're living in a system that is going through normal change or upheaval". In some cases, a minor change in one system could lead to transformation in another system. Vago (2003) confirms that it is imperative that systems, exposed to change and transformation, successfully adapt to minimise regression in society, since a collapse of one system, and the influence thereof on individuals, could have a direct influence on the success of others.

In South Africa, the term "social change" became a regularly used concept since 1990s, owing to the sociopolitical transformation that the country experienced (Bendix 2010; Nel 2012; Venter and Levy 2011). Nel (2012) emphasises that the process of change did not only intervene in the structures of the South African sociopolitical system, but also transformed its culture, defining values and overall form. The process in this transformation started with the unbanning of previously banned political organisations, including the African National Congress (ANC) and the release of Nelson Mandela on 14 February 1990. The government of the time, having already adopted a more corporatist approach, increasingly opened itself up to the major stakeholders in the political and labour sphere, as well as to other community interests. After the first democratic elections in April 1994, the

B. Linde, *The Value of Wellness in the Workplace*, SpringerBriefs in Economics,
DOI 10.1007/978-981-287-402-3_1

ANC, supported and bolstered by the Congress of South African Trade Unions (COSATU) and the South African Communist Party (SACP), assumed power as the majority party in the Government of National Unity. The newly elected government was exposed to the high expectations of its voters. Aspects that the government had to focus on included job creation for the almost 30 % unemployed, investment in the country, the dualist approach to labour relations and "the dire need for mammoth improvements and access to training and education for all South Africans" (Bendix 2010, p. 81).

A system that needed radical change after the 1994 elections was the government's approach to labour relations, which transformed from state corporatism to societal corporatism, especially through the implementation of the National Economic Development and Labour Council (Nedlac) in 1995 (Venter and Levy 2011). Bendix (2010, p. 78) states that the role of Nedlac is to endorse societal corporatism as a new approach to labour relations and to implement a demographically representative tripartite labour system in South Africa. Negotiations in Nedlac led to the development of changed labour legislation (Finnemore and Van Rensburg 2000). Grogan (2009) is of opinion that few areas of the South African law have undergone more frequent and dynamic changes in recent years than the law relating to employment. The application of the new labour legislation in organisations could imply a changing experience of the employment relationship by the employee (Linde et al. 2008).

Thus, the establishment of a societal corporatist approach to labour relations has a direct influence on other systems in the wider society. These changes also influence the employment relation, being the primary relationship between the employer, with the employer's organisations and the employee, with the labour unions, and within the labour relation system (Nel 2012). This includes the interaction processes associated with the primary relationship, individually as well as collectively, with a view to determining the conditions under which work is done so that the needs of both parties are addressed (Venter and Levy 2011).

The educational system also experienced high levels of change due to this sociopolitical transformation in South Africa (Venter and Levy 2011). Similar to the labour relations approach, before the 1994 elections, South Africa experienced a mainly dualistic approach to education (Hartshorne 1999; Nel 2012), which left a huge skills deficit between African and white South Africans. This allowed a labour market where lower level employment was mainly occupied by black South Africans and the higher level employment by white South Africans. At that stage, the South African labour relations landscape was organised and based on historical traditions of colonial rule and apartheid. Therefore, the dualism was realised through the racially separatist ideologies of the previous government and the differentiation of race groups in the regulating legislation, leading to profound inequities and distortions in the South African society (Glaser 2001; National Commission on Higher Education 1996).

Reddy (2000) describes the preparation of the South African workforce, after the 1994 elections, as follows:

> It is fragmented along racial lines, incoherent and has poor articulation between the different sectors. Under-prepared students from a poorly resourced and managed high school system result in high failure rates. Thus higher education participation rates of white and black students differ considerably being 70 % and 12 % respectively. (p. 79)

After the 1994 elections, the newly elected ANC government lived up to its principle of "equal rights to all South Africans" by replacing and changing legislation that bolstered racial separatism—including laws that controlled the mentioned dualistic educational and labour relations systems (Good 2002). A response to meet the challenges of a generally changing South Africa, and to overcome the legacy of a skewed and fragmented skills development system, is the emergence of a number of regional consortia and a range of other partnerships, regulated by new and amended labour legislation that were introduced from 1995 (Kraak 1999; Wyngaard and Kapp 2004).

1.2 South Africa's Changing Labour Relations System

Due to changes in all the socio-economic and the labour relations spheres, the South African labour market transformed since 1994. Emphasis on strategies that eliminate labour inequalities of the past and to improve general working conditions for all South Africans also appeared since 1994 with notable new and changed legislation, which aims to strengthen the labour market and address inequalities. However, with an unemployment rate that remains around 25 % from 1994, South Africa's biggest challenge remains to create jobs for semi- and unskilled labour and to develop skills for previously disadvantaged South Africans to be employed in middle and top management positions. This challenge also includes the development of a stable workforce with sustainable occupational health and safety.

South Africa is still perceived as one of the countries with the highest income inequalities in the world. This is confirmed with a World Bank Gini coefficient of 63.1 in 2009 (Worldbank 2014). This inequality actually increased since the South African sociopolitical transformation from 1994, in which the World Bank Gini coefficient was 56.6 in 1996 (Trading Economics 2014).

The influence of the transformation on the employment relationship and the employees' experience thereof will be a meaningful determent of the success of the changing labour market. The nature of the relationship between the South African organisations and its personnel is changing, due to the transformation of the labour system. Furthermore, the past experiences of the psychological contract, especially the experience of contract breach and violation, can contribute to the

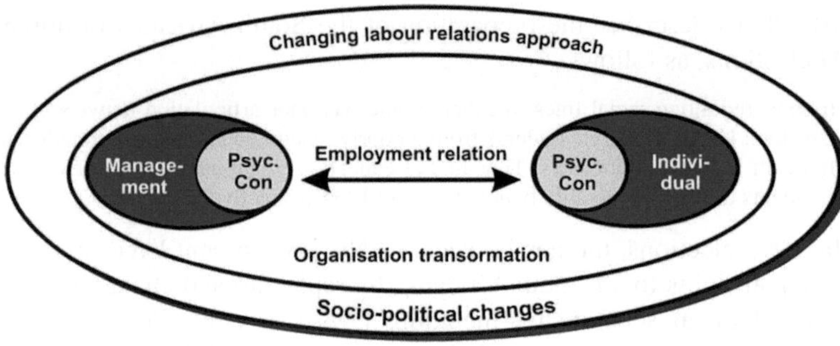

Fig. 1.1 Integrated employment relations model (adapted from Schalk and Rousseau 2001)

experience of the new labour relations in South Africa. This link can have a serious impact on the individual's work wellness, since the experience of the fairness and balance thereof has a direct influence on individual and collective wellness aspects (Linde and Schalk 2008).

Psychological contract theory is today one of the most used explication models for understanding the relationship between job insecurity and negative reactions, such as diminished loyalty, performance and general health (De Witte and Näswall 2003; King 2000; Roskies and Louis-Guerin 1990). This implies that the new employment relationship can influence the employee's psychological contract, which has short-term and long-term consequences on the employee's wellness.

Figure 1.1 indicates a model of the influence of the above-mentioned socio-political change in South Africa and the new approach to labour relations, on employment relations.

The changes in employment relations could influence the psychological contract, as experienced by the management and employees (individual). A change in the psychological contract can create job insecurity, which, as a stressor, could lead to lower levels of job satisfaction and could have an impact on the wellness of employees. Thus, in a sociopolitical changed environment with a new labour relation approach, the transformation of the labour relations landscape in South Africa can have a direct influence on the workplace wellness of the employees. In particular, the employees in semi- and unskilled positions can experience a changing psychological contract, due to new employment legislation and conditions, which can influence the employee's experience of job security and satisfaction, and general health. This experience of work wellness will influence the organisational structures and has a direct impact on the management processes.

The mentioned model was focused on the employment relationship and the influence of the individual's and the employer's characteristics on this relationship, as well as the sociopolitical and labour relations changes. It does not note the important influence of collective and normative actions and approaches to the individual relationship, which can be linked to a social context that includes employer and employee organisations. These collective influences are part of the broader employee–organisation relationship, which is not only including the legal and psychological contracts between an individual and employer, but also the influence of social and normative contracts. These broader influences also have an impact on the work-related wellness.

1.3 The Employee-Organisation Relationship and Wellness

This psychological contract is used as an explication model with the employee's experience of job insecurity, job satisfaction and general health, perceived as work wellness. Work-related stress is costly in terms of human suffering and financial costs, and the amount of individuals experiencing stress is growing internationally. Stress, in the majority of stress theories and models, is described as a series of factors that have their beginning in one's actual surroundings and conclude with the individual's reactions (Hellgren 2003). The individual forms a concept of the objective situation through the subjective interpretation of the situation. Through this process, individuals determine the situation's significance and therefore stress can be characterised as a process in which individuals interact with their surroundings (Beehr 1998). This approach to stress in the employee–organisation relationship has a prominent individual character, with limited focus on the relational impact and reactions.

As illustrated in Fig. 1.2, Hellgren (2003, p. 24) describes the stress process as that in which the individual creates a subjective or psychological conception of the objective reality, and it is this subjective interpretation which then triggers reactions—of a physiological, psychological and behavioural nature—that finally, in the last stage of this process, result in the development of mental and physical health complaints. Hellgren (2003) also indicates the focus of social context on the changes of objective conditions to subjective experience.

The stress process model has a balanced focus on wellness, where the individual's characteristics are not the only influence, but where the social context is also

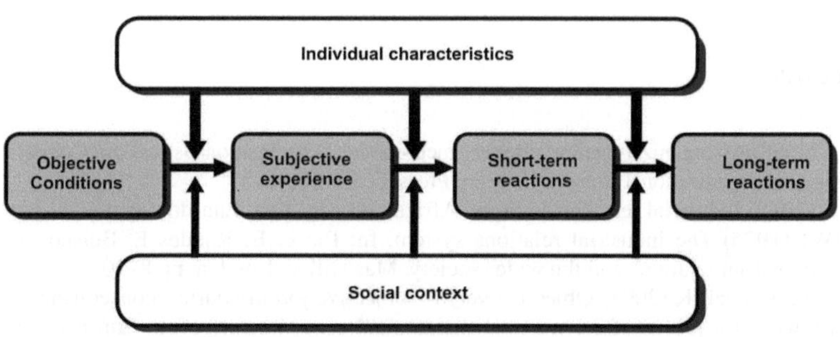

Fig. 1.2 Adapted stress process model of Katz and Kahn (1978) (Hellgren 2003)

considered. It is important to take in account the social context in work-related wellness, where normative (group association, e.g. trade union membership) and social (e.g. economic situation and inequalities) influences can have a big influence on the individual's well-being. This model also includes the difference between short- and long-term reactions.

With the sociopolitical change and a changing approach to labour relations in South Africa, a huge demand for successful adaptation is placed on organisations, which could influence the wellness of the personnel. The social context changes that the employees experience therefore include the transformation process, as well as the changing South African labour relations approach. The management process within the organisations is also a component of the social context in which the transformation is experienced by the employee. Such management structures include employment-related codes, policies and procedures. Subjective experiences of these social context influences on the employees' objective conditions (e.g. the employment relationship) include the experience of clarity of the employment regulations, trust in these regulations and the experience of the psychological contract. This experience of the psychological contract, and especially the experience of breach and violation of the contract, can influence the experience of job satisfaction and job insecurity as short-term reactions, which can lead to a long-term reaction in terms of the employee's well-being, including general health (Hellgren 2003). These relational influences on individual's work wellness will also have a direct impact on the organisation's structures and viability. The focus of this book was to investigate the dynamics of wellness in the workplace and the economic cost thereof.

The link between the employee–organisation relations (EOR)—the employment relationship and the psychological contract—and the economic value of wellness—individual and relational—is investigated in this book. First (Chap. 2), the psychological contract is discussed, including the impact thereof on individual wellness. Thereafter (Chap. 3), the employment relationship, as part of the EOR, is investigated from a South African context. Chapter 4 focusses on the economic value of wellness in the workplace, where the individual and relational impacts are investigated. Chapter 5, in conclusion, will propose a framework of the influence of the EOR on work wellness, including the economic value thereof.

References

Beehr TA (1998) An organizational psychology meta-model of occupational stress. In: Cooper CL (ed) Theories of organizational stress. University Press, Oxford, pp 6–27

Bendix S (2010) Industrial relations in South Africa, 5th edn. Juta, Lansdowne

Craig AWJ (1975) The industrial relations system. In: Barret B, Rhodes E, Beishon Collier J (eds) Industrial relations and the wider society. MacMillan, London, pp 8–20

De Witte H, Näswall K (2003) Objective versus subjective job insecurity: consequences of temporary work for job satisfaction and organizational commitment in four European countries. Econ Ind Democracy 24:147–186

Dunlop JT (1993) Industrial relations systems (Rev. ed). Harvard Business School Press, Boston

Fink S (2001) Standards and whole system change. Teaching and Change 237–248
Finnemore M, Van Rensburg R (2000) Contemporary labour relations. Butterworths, Durban
Glaser D (2001) Politics and society in South Africa: a critical introduction. Sage, London
Good K (2002) The liberal model and Africa: elites against democracy. Palgrave, New York
Grogan J (2009) Workplace law, 10th edn. Juta, Kenwyn
Hartshorne KB (1999) The making of education policy in South Africa. Oxford, Cape Town
Hellgren J (2003) The times they are a-changin': job uncertainty and the flexible labor market. Akademitryck, Edsbruk
Katz D, Kahn RL (1978) The social psychology of organisations, 2nd edn. Wiley, New York
King JE (2000) White-collar reactions to job insecurity and the role of the psychological contract: implications for human resource management. Hum Resour Manage 39:79–91
Kraak N (1999) Investigating new knowledge production: a South African higher education case study. Paper presented at the University of Massachusetts, Amherst
Linde B, Schalk R, Linde HM (2008) Clarity and trust: the experience of workplace regulations by employees. S Afr J Labour Relat 32(2):86–103
Linde B, Schalk R (2008) The influence of pre-merger employment relations and individual characteristics on the psychological contract: a South African case study. S Afr J Psychol 38(2):305–320
National Commission on Higher Education (1996) A framework for transformation. Final report, Republic of South Africa. Government Press, Pretoria
Nel PS (2012) South African employment relations: theory and practice, 7th edn. Van Schaik Publishers, Pretoria
Reddy J (2000) Regional consortia, partnerships, mergers and implications for the transformation of the South African higher education system. S Afr J High Educ 14:79–87
Roskies E, Lewis-Guerin C (1990) Job insecurities in managers: antecedents and consequences. J Organ Behav 14:617–630
Schalk R, Rousseau DM (2001) Psychological contracts in employment. In: Anderson N (ed) Handbook of industrial, work and organizational psychology. Sage, London, pp 133–142
Sztompka P (1991) Society in action: the theory of social becoming. Polity Press, Cambridge
Toeffler A (1999) Shock talk. Hosp Health Netw 73:28
Trading Economics (2014) GINI index in South Africa. http://www.tradingeconomics.com/south-africa/gini-index-wb-data.html. Retrieved from 25 Feb 2014
Vago S (2003) Social change, 5th edn. Prentice Hall, New York
Venter R, Levy A (eds) (2011) Labour relations in South Africa, 3rd ed. Oxford University Press, Cape Town
Worldbank (2014) Data: the GINI index. http://data.worldbank.org/indicator/SI.POV.GINI. Retrieved from 25 Feb 2014
Wyngaard A, Kapp C (2004) Rethinking and reimagining mergers in further and higher education: a human perspective. S Afr J High Educ 18:185–201

Chapter 2
The Psychological Contract

2.1 The Psychological Contract as Part of the Employee-Organisation Relationship (EOR)

The individual does not operate in isolation at work. The dynamics of social interactions in the workplace have an important influence on the experience of work wellness and the success of the organisation. According to Blyton and Turnbull (1998, p. 3), "work dominates the lives of most men and women, and the management of employees, both individually and collectively, remains a central feature of organisational life". Hellgren (2003) elaborates on this and emphasises the influence of work, and workplace relations, on the wellness of the employee, the employer and their environment.

The influences at work and the management of work form a dynamic and complex system, involving various parties, structures and regulations (Salamon 1998), encompassing both the direct working environment ("microenvironment") and the wider society ("macroenvironment"; Venter and Levy 2011, p. 18). Labour relations, and especially the relationship between employees and employers, play an important role in the dynamics of the wider society (Craig 1975).

The employee–organisation relationship (EOR) is the pivotal relationship in the labour relations system, since the individual relationships between the employees and their employers are the origin of the complexity and dynamics of the total

---

Chapter Aim The aim of this chapter is to investigate the role of the psychological contract as part of the employee–organisation relationship (EOR). The influence of the experience of contract breach and violation on the wellness of individuals will also be discussed.

The focus of this book is on work-related wellness and its value. This wellness does not only refer to the individual's experience, but also refer to the work-related relational wellness. Chapter 3 will focus on the relational wellness, while this chapter investigates the role of the psychological contract with more individual wellness in a work context.

B. Linde, *The Value of Wellness in the Workplace*, SpringerBriefs in Economics,
DOI 10.1007/978-981-287-402-3_2

system (Bendix 2010; Salamon 1998; Tustin and Geldenhuys 2000). Shore et al. (2004) give an overview of various concepts that have been studied in relation to the EOR, including the psychological contract (Rousseau 1995), perceived organisational support (Eisenberger et al. 1986), leader member exchange (Graen and Uhl-Bien 1995) and the employment relationship (Shore et al. 2004). Research on the EOR has increased substantially in the past decade, especially with respect to research on psychological contracts (e.g. Hellgren 2003; Herriot and Pemberton 1996; McLean Parks et al. 1998; Pugh et al. 2003; Rousseau 1995, 2001; Schalk and Rousseau 2001) and employment relationships (Shore et al. 2004).

According to Shore et al. (2004, p. 296), there are four reasons why there is a focus on the psychological contract and employment relationships as important constructs of the EOR:

- both constructs focus on exchange, highlighting the importance of examining both parties' (employee's and organisation's) perceptions of the relationship;
- psychological contract research has focused on the individual perspective, and employment relationship literature on the group or organisational perspective;
- both concepts have inspired a great deal of research; and
- there are similarities and differences in the ways of synthesising the literatures on these constructs in the EOR domain.

In this chapter, the psychological contract will be highlighted, and in Chap. 3, the employment relationship, both as concepts of the EOR, since the identification and implementation of employment rules (explicit regulations), as experienced by the employee, are identified by the psychological contract, and their maintenance and implementation are controlled by the employment relationship. It is important to note that these two concepts cannot be wholly separated from each other. Guest (2004), for example, is of the opinion that the psychological contract constructs need extending to give greater weight to the "state" of the psychological contract, *incorporating* issues of fairness and trust that lie at the heart of employment relations.

The psychological contract and the employment relationship are discussed separately, taking the interdependence of the constructs into account.

Labour relations, with the EOR as the core relationship, play an essential role in society's economy and are closely related to the social welfare, political, legal, environmental, religious and educational spheres (Katz and Kochan 2000). The context of the societal environment brings about changes in labour relations that are experienced on both the macro- and the microenvironmental levels. Such changes, which are most visible in organisational transformations (including acquisitions and mergers), have a direct influence on the EOR and on employee wellness.

Since the early 1990s, interest in the concept of the psychological has grown tremendously, even though the concept was already introduced in 1960 by Argyris (1960). Levinson, Price, Munden, Mandl and Solley further elaborated on this concept in 1962 by identifying the psychological contract as an exchange relationship between employer and employee in which each party has expectations about mutual obligations. The psychological contract, defined as the set of practical and emotional expectations of benefits that employers and employees can reasonably have of each other, was traditionally seen as an exchange of loyalty for security. However, as Hiltrop (1995) notes, "the psychological contract that gave security, stability and predictability to the relationship between employees and employers has dramatically altered in the past decades" (p. 286).

The definitions that enjoy current prominence tend to emphasise the importance of the subjective understanding and experience of the individual employee (McLean Parks et al. 1998). According to Rousseau (1995), the psychological contract includes "individual beliefs, shaped by the organisation, regarding terms of an exchange agreement between individuals and their organisation" (p. 9). These individual beliefs refer to expectations and obligations based on perceived promises. With regard to the employment relationship, Isaksson et al. (2003) define the psychological contract as "the perception of reciprocal expectations and obligations implied in the employment relationship" (p. 3). It must be noted that reference to the psychological contract usually refers to the *employee's* experience of perceived promises, in the form of employee and employer obligations. Technically, however, the psychological contract is of a reciprocal nature, where the employer also participates in the experience of the psychological contract.

From the above-mentioned statements, a combined formal definition can be derived:

> The psychological contract is the experience of employee and employer obligations through perceived promises made in the reciprocal employee–organisation relationship.

These expectations are not limited to the psychological contract only and are also integrated in the EOR through other influences, including the social and legal contracts (Shore et al. 2004).

The EOR, as the comprehensive relationship between the individual employee and the organisation, forms and operates in societies with specific societal and legal contexts. The societal context is reflected in the ***social contract***: statements of obligations logically arising from a specific kind of societal relationship (Kary 2000). Rousseau (1995) states that the "social contract refers to cultural collective beliefs regarding appropriate behaviour in society" (p. 13). This identifies the social contract as a normative framework to resolve ethical dilemmas (Shore et al. 2004). In a labour-related perspective, this framework refers to internationally agreed best practices, including the International Labour Organisation's (ILO's) conventions and recommendations, as well as national labour legislation (Grogan 2009).

Employment contracts within the society must comply with the social contract to be considered as legitimate. Traditionally, such a ***legal contract*** will comprise the application of rigid rules, the formal promises in return for agreed obligations, objective evidence of an offer, an acceptance and the exchange of valuable consideration, and the agreement of being a static contract with terms that were fixed at the moment of formation (Eisenberg 2001). Shore et al. (2004) refer to the modern interpretation of contract law by recognising obligations as based on both promissory and non-promissory principles, as well as recognising the uniqueness of the individual relationship, and the subjectivity of the contract.

The perspective of a legal contract also takes the flexibility and individuality of an agreement into account and acknowledges that rigidity and total objectivity (reasonable person standard) in the contract is not always viable (Eisenberg 2001). When referring to employment contracts, the general reaction is that they entail only this, usually written, legal contract. Actually, employment contracts are also based on the aforementioned social contract and will include normative and implicit contracts.

Shore et al. (2004, p. 301) state that above-mentioned contracts (social and legal contracts), next to the influence of interorganisation group beliefs (the ***normative contract***) and implied-in-fact perceived promises (the ***implied contract***), are also the main contributing factors of the individual psychological contract that, on its own, establishes the foundation of the EOR. As illustrated by Rousseau (1995, p. 9; Table 2.1), psychological and implied contracts are experienced on an individual and personal level by the employee, while the normative, legal and social contracts are related to group levels of experience.

The social, legal and normative contracts are closely associated with the social context influences (as later discussed) on the employment relationships. Since the influences on the psychological contract are constantly changing, because of, for example, political transformation and amendments to labour laws, the EOR is also continuously exposed to a changing environment. To accommodate these influences and to avoid the experience of violation of the psychological contract, perceived organisation support, LMX and the other characteristics of the employment relationship play an important role (Shore et al. 2004). For purposes of this chapter, however, the focus will be limited to the psychological contract and the employment relationship's influence on it.

This model differentiates between individual and relational experiences. This is valuable to wellness studies, where the individual and relational—collective—influences are incorporated. The role of individual and collective, as well as formal and informal, contracts on wellness experiences will be investigated later in this book (Chap. 4).

Table 2.1 Contracts influencing the psychological contract

	Collective	Individual
Formal	*Social Contract*	*Legal contract*
	• ILO conventions • Societal norms • Constitution • Labour legislation • Collective agreements	• Written/verbal employment contract • Idiosyncratic deals
Informal	*Normative contract*	*Implicit contract*
	• Professional status • Generally accepted job behaviour • Group norms • Subculture norms	• Personality-type behaviour • Cultural background • Physical characteristics • Literacy levels

Source Adapted from Rousseau (1995, p. 9)

2.2 Breach and Violation of the Psychological Contract

Concerning breach and violation of the psychological contract, Rousseau (1995) states the following:

> In the strictest sense, violation refers to a failure to comply with the terms of a contract. But, given the subjective nature of the psychological contract, how people interpret the circumstances of this failure determines whether they experience a violation. (p. 112)

Therefore, a violation of the psychological contract refers to emotional and affective reactions such as those that may arise when the individual feels that the organisation failed to uphold properly its end of the psychological contract, for whatever reason (Morrison and Robertson 1997). More specifically, a "violation of the psychological contract arises when the employee perceives a discrepancy between perceived obligations and promised obligations" (Schalk et al. 2001, p. 7). There can be various reasons why the employer does not comply with promised obligations to the employee. Rousseau (1995) identifies three sources of experienced violation, "inadvertent experience, disruption and breach of contract" (p. 112). The sources of the experience of violation determine the ability and willingness of the employer to comply with the promised obligations to the employee.

Table 2.2 identifies the sources and characteristics of experienced violation, according to Rousseau (1995), and possible examples thereof. Several researchers (e.g. Atkinson 2002; Lemire and Rouillard 2005; Newell and Dopson 1996) see breach of contract as a form of violation, rather than a cause. They associate a certain level of experience of violation with a specific reason. These researchers mainly refer to breach of contract as associated with the experience of violation, rather than taking other reasons into account. The intensity of the experience of violation, however, could not yet be directly associated with its source. Therefore, an employee's level of experience of violation due to a merger of organisations (the cause being *disruption*) can be similar to an employee's experiencing violation due to unfair labour practice, e.g. fewer rewards than promised (the cause being *breach of contract*). This implies that even though the employer wants to deliver the promises made, but is unable to do it due to external reasons, the

Table 2.2 Sources of experienced violation

Source	Characteristics	Examples
Inadvertent	Able and willing (divergent interpretations made in good faith)	Misunderstanding of promise or detail, e.g. employee accidentally at wrong place of work
Disruption	Willing, but unable (inability to fulfil contract)	Operational requirements, due to financial, structural or technological reasons, e.g. a forced merger
Breach of contract	Able, but unwilling (reneging)	Unilateral changes of contract without fair reason or process, e.g. substantive unfair dismissal

Source Adapted from Rousseau (1995, p. 113)

employee can experience violation of contract. Some of the most recent research in the experience of violation focuses on breach of contract (Atkinson 2002; Lemire and Rouillard 2005; Searle and Ball 2004), while the experience of violation can be the same, whatever the source.

Due to regular use of the term, "breach of contact", referring to partial or all sources of experience of violation (Atkinson 2002; Lemire and Rouillard 2005; Morrison and Robertson 1997; Searle and Ball 2004), in this chapter, this term will subsequently also be used in this way. This implies that for the purpose of this chapter "breach of contract" refers to the action of the employer not to keep a promise made for whatever reason, as perceived by the employee, and "violation of contract" refers to the employee's emotional and affective reactions to the experience of breach of contract, for whatever reason. The employee's experience of breach and violation of contract is therefore mainly based on how the employee perceives promises made and kept by the employer.

Indicators and reactions of the experience of contract breach and violation are not only visible in individual short-term reactions (including experience of job satisfaction and job insecurity) and long-term reactions (including employee well-being and general health; Ferrie et al. 1995; Hellgren 2003; Roskies et al. 1993), but also include labour-related actions, such as high levels of absenteeism, lodging of organisational grievances by the employee, referring disputes by the employee, industrial actions (protected or unprotectedindustrial actions) and strong union activities (Bendix 2010; Nel 2012; Venter and Levy 2011).

2.3 Employee and Employer Obligations

The content of the psychological contract refers to the concrete terms that are part of the perceived relationship (Rousseau and Tijouriwala 1998). These concrete terms are embodied by employee and employer obligations, as perceived by the parties in the EOR. The range and level at which these obligations are perceived are guided by the social, legal, normative and implicit contracts (as previously discussed) that the employee is exposed to. As an example, an employee with a vague legal employment contract may easily perceive more employer obligations than an employee with a clear legal contract. This might lead to an elevated experience of breach and violation of contract by the employee, since the perceived employer obligation may not be similar to how the employer perceives the obligation.

The range of perceived obligations can be unlimited, due to the above-mentioned contractual influences on the psychological contract, causing difficulty in identifying specific employee and employer obligations. Using a limited subset of items for which scales are developed, researchers face the problem that no consensus is reached on which scales and items to use (De Vos et al. 2002; Van Den Brande 2002). A broad scale of psychological contract content can be identified through classifications by Robinson et al. (1994), De Vos et al. (2002), as summarised in Table 2.3 (as cited in PSYCONES 2005, p. 16).

Employer and employee obligations, as perceived by the employee, can be based on various promises made to the employer, as well as promises made by the employer to the employee. The range of perceived promises is unlimited and can differ significantly between various forms of employment, industries and sectors,

Table 2.3 Content of the psychological contract

Obligations of the employee		Obligations of the employer
Robinson et al. (1994)	De Vos et al. (2002)	De Vos et al. (2002)
Working overtime	Job performance	Job content
Loyalty	Flexibility	Opportunities for career development
Extra-role behaviour	Extra-role behaviour	Social aspects
Notice	Loyalty	Support
Transfers	Employability	Rewards
Competitor support	Ethics	Respect for private life
Proprietary protection		
Minimum stay		

Source Adapted from PSYCONES (2005, p. 16)

Table 2.4 Psychological contract obligations and promises guideline

Employee obligations	Employee promises	Employer obligations	Employer promises
Job performance	Good service	Job content	Varied work
	Professional manner		Limited disturbances
	General honesty		Own work fashion
	Skills development		Responsibility
	Satisfying performance		Right to supervise
	Team player		Right of own opinion
			Departmental influence
Loyalty	Protect organizational image	Rewards	Flexibility
	Confidentiality		Fair salary
	Not support competitors		Job security
Ethics	Honesty with leave		Additional rewards
	Resignation notice		Allowances
	Cost-effective		Recognition
Extra-role behaviour	Respect company time	Management policy	Procedural fairness
	Innovation		Fair discipline
	Assist others		Communication structures
	Social participation		Information

(continued)

Table 2.4 (continued)

Employee obligations	Employee promises	Employer obligations	Employer promises
Flexibility	Accept transfer	Social aspects	Co-employee relationships
	Do non-required tasks		Supporting social activities
	Work extra hours		Colleague assistance
	Geographical mobility		Good working atmosphere
			Social network
	Conformity	Career development	Reaching true potential
			Stimulating work
			Room for own initiatives
			Suitable work
			Ability to achieve progress
			Promotion abilities
			Skills development
			Horizontal job mobility
			Training opportunities
			Fair work pressure
		Organisational support	Quality products
			Customer satisfaction
			Feedback
			Righteous management
			Trust in management
			Efficient organisation
			Good working conditions
			Good HRM
			Fair work time
			Reimbursement of costs
			Respect for private life

Source Linde et al. (2008)

occupations and professions, workplaces and personality characteristics, to name but a few. A proposed guideline of types of employee and employer obligations, with the associated types of promises, has been compiled in Table 2.4, through adaptations of relevant sources (De Vos et al. 2002; PSYCONES 2005; Rousseau and Tijouriwala 1998; Van Den Brande 2002).

Owing to the subjective character of the psychological contract, the perceived promises and obligations associated with the uniqueness of each employment relationship and the structuring thereof can only be seen as a guideline, rather than a fixed scale. Furthermore, certain promises can be identified as part of more than one obligation, depending on the situation in which they are made and/or perceived. Table 2.4 has therefore been specifically developed and structured in the context of South African-based research into the contents of the psychological contract, by Linde et al. (2008).

2.4 Influence of the Social Context on the Psychological Contract

As illustrated in Fig. 1.1, both the individual's characteristics and the social context associated with the EOR can influence the employee's experience of the psychological contract and employment relationship, as well as the following short-term reactions (e.g. job insecurity and job satisfaction) and long-term reactions (e.g. employee well-being and general health; Hellgren 2003; Hellgren et al. 1999). These individual characteristics can include the employee's personality characteristics, age, gender, emotional intelligence, literacy level and ability to understand—characteristics that have a prominent influence on the individual's formation of an implicit contract and which therefore also influence the psychological contract (Guest 2004; Rousseau 1995), as indicated in Table 2.1.

The psychological contract is also reciprocally related with the social, legal and normative contracts, which are sensitive to the social context in which they are formed and sustained. This social context can include the sociopolitical situation of a country or area, the demographic composition, levels of industrial development, societal norms, labour and other legislation, organisational culture and employment regulations and rules (Bendix 2010; Venter and Levy 2011). Therefore, the characteristics of an employment relationship can be entrenched by the direct social context influences to which it is exposed. As an example, employment relationships in the same sector and demographic area can be very different due to the management structures, organisational culture and collective bargaining processes of the organisation. The employees associated with these different employment relationships can experience different psychological contracts, as well as different breaches and violations of these contracts. The short-term and long-term reactions associated with these different experiences of the psychological contract can lead to very diverse wellness levels in the workforce.

Two main groups of social context influences on the employment relationship can be identified, namely external and internal. The external influences are beyond the reasonable control of the organisation (including labour law, sectoral determinations, national economic policies, the labour market and natural resources), and the internal influences are within the organisation's reasonable control (including organisational and management policies and structures, employment regulations, negotiation processes, personnel relationships and performance policies). Where different types of employment relationships operate under the same labour legislation and in the same labour sector, the internal social context becomes the primary cause for diverse relationships (Venter and Levy 2011).

The employment relationship, exposed to these influences, therefore has unique characteristics, causing the employer and employee to experience the psychological contract in context. The influences that the social context can have on the employment relationship will mostly be realised in the management system of the relationship (Tustin and Geldenhuys 2000), which comprises organisational rules and regulations and their application (Bendix 2010). Therefore, the clarity and consistency of the employment relationship, as experienced by the employee, are dictated by the contents, communication and fairness of employment-related contracts, policies, codes and procedures implemented by the employer (Nel 2012; Venter and Levy 2011). These employment relationship characteristics influence the employee's experience of employee and employer obligations, owing to the clarity of the mentioned promises made and the employee's trust in the employer to keep them.

The experience of the psychological contract clearly links to the employment relationship. Thus, the employees' wellness influences their state of the psychological contract, which also has an influence on the experience of the employment relationship. The dynamics of the employment relationship is discussed in the following chapter, where the changing labour relationships of South Africa are also discussed.

References

Argyris C (1960) Understanding organizational behaviour. Dorsey Press, Homewood

Atkinson C (2002) Career management and the changing psychological contract. Career Develop Int 7(1):14–23

Bendix S (2010) Industrial relations in South Africa, 7th edn. Juta, Lansdowne

Blyton P, Turnbull P (1998) The dynamics of employee relations, 2nd edn. MacMillan, Basingstoke, United Kingdom

Craig AWJ (1975) The industrial relations system. In: Barret B, Rhodes E, Beishon Collier J (eds) Industrial relations and the wider society. MacMillan, London, pp 8–20

De Vos J, Buyens D, Schalk R (2002) Psychological contract-related information seeking and the role of individual disposition. Poster accepted for the annual conference of the Society of Industrial and Organizational Psychology, Toronto, Canada

Eisenberg MA (2001) Contracts and property law: the emergence of dynamic contract law. Theor Inq Law 2:1–76

Eisenberger R, Huntington R, Hutchison S, Sowa D (1986) Perceived organizational support. J Appl Psychol 71:500–507

Ferrie JE, Shipley M, Marmot MG, Stansfield S, Davey-Smith G (1995) Health effects of anticipation of change and non-employment longitudinal data from the Whitehall II study. Br Med J 311:1264–1269

Graen GB, Uhl-Bien M (1995) Relationship-based approach to leadership: development of Leader-member exchange (LMX) theory of leadership over 25 years. Leadersh Quart 6:219–247

Grogan J (2009) Workplace law, 9th edn. Juta, Kenwyn

Guest D (2004) The psychology of the employment relationship: an analysis based on the psychological contract. Appl Psychol 53:541–555

Hellgren J (2003) The times they are a-changin': job uncertainty and the flexible labor market. Akademitryck, Edsbruk

Hellgren J, Sverke M, Isaksson K (1999) A two-dimensional approach to job insecurity: consequences for employee attitudes and well-being. Eur J Work Organ Psychol 8:179–195

Herriot P, Pemberton C (1996) Contracting careers. Hum Relat 49:757–790

Hiltrop JM (1995) The changing psychological contract: the human resource challenge of the 1990s. Eur Manag J 13:286–294

Isaksson K, Bernhard C, Gustafsson K (2003) Betydelse av anställningsform och tillit till ledningen för personalens halsa inom vården [Importance of employment form and trust into leadership for employee's health in the healthcare sector]. Arbetsmarknad Arbetsliv 9(2):5–16

Kary JH (2000) Contract law and the social contract: what legal history can teach us about the political theory of Hobbes and Locke. Univ Ottawa Law Rev 31:73–91

Katz H, Kochan T (2000) An introduction to collective bargaining and industrial relationships, 2nd edn. McGraw-Hill, Boston

Lemire L, Rouillard C (2005) An empirical exploration of psychological contract violation and individual behaviour: the case of Canadian federal civil servants in Quebec. J Manage Psychol 20:150–163

Levinson H, Price CR, Munden KJ, Mandl HJ, Solley CM (1962) Men, management and mental health. Harvard University Press, Cambridge

Linde B, Schalk R, Linde HM (2008) Clarity and trust: the experience of workplace regulations by employees. South Afr J Labour Relat 32(2):86–103

McLean Parks J, Kidder DL, Gallagher DG (1998) Fitting square pegs into round holes: mapping the domain of contingent work arrangements onto the psychological contract. J Organ Behav 19:697–730

Morrison EW, Robinson SL (1997) When employees feel betrayed: a model of how psychological contract violation develops. Acad Manage Rev 1:226–256

Nel PS (2012) South African employment relations: theory and practice, 7th edn. Van Schaik, Pretoria

Newell H, Dopson S (1996) Muddle in the middle: organizational restructuring and middle management careers. Pers Rev 25(4):4–20

PSYCONES (2005) WP1—state of the art: current evidence concerning employment contracts and employee/organizational well-being among workers in Europe. http://www.psycones.sp. Retrieved 11 Nov 2005

Pugh SD, Scarlicki DP, Passell BS (2003) After the fall: layoff victims' trust and cynicism in re-employment. J Occup Organ Psychol 76:201–213

Robinson SL, Kraatz MS, Rousseau DM (1994) Changing obligations and the psychological contract: a longitudinal study. Acad Manage J 37(1):137–152

Roskies E, Lewis-Guerin C, Fournier C (1993) Coping with job insecurity: how does personality make a difference? J Organ Behav 14:617–630

Rousseau DM (1995) Psychological contracts in organizations: understanding written and unwritten agreements. Sage, Thousand Oaks

Rousseau DM (2001) Schema, promise and mutuality: the building blocks of the psychological contract. J Occup Organ Psychol 74:511–541

Rousseau DM, Tijouriwala SA (1998) Assessing psychological contracts: issues, alternatives and measures. J Organ Behav 19:679–695

Salamon M (1998) Industrial relations: theory and practice, 3rd edn. Prentice Hall, Hertfordshire

Schalk R, Heinen J, Freese C (2001) Do organizational changes impact the psychological contract and workplace attitudes? a study of a merger of two home care organizations in the Netherlands. In: De Jonge J, Vlerick P, Büssing A, Schaufeli WB (eds) Organizational psychology and health care at the start of a new millennium. Rainer Hampp Verlag, Munich

Schalk R, Rousseau DM (2001) Psychological contracts in employment. In: Anderson N (ed) Handbook of industrial, work and organizational psychology. Sage, London, pp 133–142

Searle RH, Ball KS (2004) The development of trust and distrust in a merger. J Manage Psychol 19:708–721

Shore LM, Tetrick LE, Taylor S, Shapiro JA-MC, Liden R, Parks JM, Morrison EW, Porter LW, Robinson S, Roehling MV, Rousseau DM, Schalk R, Tsui A, Van Dyne L (2004) The employee-organization relationship: a timely concept in a period of transition. In: Martocchio JJ (ed) Research in personnel and human resources management, vol 23. Elsevier, Oxford, pp 291–370

Tustin C, Geldenhuys D (2000) Labour relations: the psychology of conflict and negotiation. Oxford University Press, Cape Town

Van den Brande I (2002) Het psychologish contract tussen werknemer en werkgever: een survey-onderzoek by vlaamse werknemers [The psychological contract between employee and employer: a survey with Flemish employees]. Unpublished mater's thesis, Katholieke Universiteit Leuven, Leuven

Venter R, Levy A (eds) (2011) Labour relations in South Africa, 3rd edn. Oxford University Press, Cape Town

Chapter 3
The Employment Relationship

3.1 The Employment Relationship as Part of the Labour Relations System

The labour relationship, initially defined by Dunlop (1958) as the industrial relationship, identifies the employment relationship between the individual employee and employer as the pivotal relation in the functioning of the broader labour relations system (Salamon 1998). It is therefore safe to assume that the complexity of this conception, being the employment relationship, cannot be wholly exposed through a definition only. To identify and discuss the concept of employment relations, or, more precisely, "the management of interactions between the employer and the employee" (Venter and Levy 2011, p. 4), this relationship should be analysed in the context of the broader labour relations system and its intricate functioning, exposing the various levels and intensity of relations associated with labour (Craig 1975; Nel 2012).

J.T. Dunlop originated the application of the systems concept to labour relations in 1958 (Salamon 1998, p. 12), while initially mainly focusing on rules in labour relations, the reasons why particular rules are established in specific labour relationships and the changeableness of these rules (Bendix 2010; Dunlop 1958; Tustin and Geldenhuys 2000; Venter and Levy 2011). These initial objectives directed Dunlop (1958) into an integrated model, where the influence of the environment on labour relations, and vice versa, was taken in account. In this labour relations system approach, Dunlop (1958) sought to "provide tools of analysis to interpret and gain understanding of the widest possible range of labour relations facts and practices" (p. vi).

Chapter Aim The aim of this chapter is to investigate the employment relationship as part of the EOR from a South African context.

B. Linde, *The Value of Wellness in the Workplace*, SpringerBriefs in Economics,
DOI 10.1007/978-981-287-402-3_3

To achieve these objectives, Dunlop (1958) referred to "actors" in the relationship, the context of the labour relationship, ideology and rules. The "***actors***" referred to the employee, employer and state, with their separate representatives. In the case of Dunlop's model, the actors do not refer to individuals, but more collective groups, since the model's objective focused on "widest possible range of labour relations facts and practices" (Dunlop 1958, p. vi; Finnemore 1999, p. 4).

Referring to the ***context*** of the labour relations system, Dunlop (1958, p. 9) focussed on the influence of demand and supply in the labour market, and their subsequent power to the labour "seller" or "buyer". This context also refers to the power base within society and the technological environment (Tustin and Geldenhuys 2000). The influences of ideology refer, according to Dunlop (1958), to the political frame of reference of the society in which the labour relations system operates, as well as the parties participating therein. In this case, certain activities, and the reasons therefor, of one party in the labour relations system may conflict with another party's. Through the interaction of the parties ("actors") of the labour relations system and its context and ideologies, ***rules*** are developed that regulate the interaction in the system (Venter and Levy 2011). These regulations refer to labour legislation, as well as to more specific employment regulations. These forms of regulations are discussed later on in this chapter, in order to achieve the research objectives.

With the development of the labour relations system theory, Craig (1975) published an article, titled: "A framework for the analysis of industrial relations systems". In this paper, Craig (1975, p. 18) expanded the constructs of Dunlop's original labour relations system model, by elaborating on the influence of system inputs and outputs, mechanisms for converting these inputs and outputs, the feedback loops (for both when the labour relations mechanism operates successful, as well as for breakdowns in the mechanism) and identifying specific environmental systems influencing the labour relations system. Through these adaptations, the process of developing regulations in the labour relations system takes the influence of other systems into account more actively, as well as the influence of these regulations on the broader society. The process of developing these regulations is also elaborated on, taking into account the:

- "…day-to-day interpersonal relations to satisfy individual goals;
- structure of negotiation units;
- collective bargaining, grievance procedures, continuous committee, etc.;
- conciliation;
- commissions of inquiry;
- arbitration of interest disputes; and
- strikes" (Craig 1975, p. 19).

Craig's (1975) contribution to the labour relations system theory is mainly focussing on the societal role of the subsystems and the interdependence between them, rather than isolating the labour relations system. This elaboration of Dunlop's (1958) original model is an aspect which was originally criticised (Lumley 1974). The model was not changed by Craig, but the interaction process in the development of labour regulations was better identified, as well as its influence on, and in, rule-making.

Further contributions to the labour relations system theory include those by Wood et al. (1975) and, more recently, Salamon (1998). These writers identify and question the objective of the labour relations system. The crucial issue, in their view, is whether the central feature of the labour relations system should be the rules (output) or the rule-making (process) (Salamon 1998, p. 13). Through this criticism, an analytical distinction can be drawn between the "system which 'produces' rules and the system which is governed by these rules" (Wood et al. 1975, p. 295). Salamon (1998) identified a follow-up framework for distinguishing between:

- "rules which are an output from the industrial (labour) relations system to 'govern' behaviour within the production system (substantive rules and, possibly procedural rules for regulating the interpretation and application of substantive rules); and
- rules which are established for internal regulation of the industrial relations system (procedural)" (p. 13).

These forms of rules are discussed later on in this chapter, with the former as *implicit regulations* and the latter as *explicit regulations*. Through the contributions of the latter writers, the focus increasingly fell on the individual relationship and the process in which the governing rules are implemented and managed, in contrast to the initial models of Dunlop (1958) and Craig (1975).

Employment relations deal essentially with people who, because of their mutual involvement in the working environment, have been placed in a specific relationship with one another (Bendix 2010). The employment relationship is not only the focus of labour relations on the specific employee–employer relationship, but it also forms the basis of human resource management (Slabbert and Swanepoel 2001). Therefore, employment relations are a combination of labour relations management and human resource management, within the individual relationship between the employee and employer (Shore et al. 2004).

Labour relations management deals with decision-making and behaviour regarding aspects such as trade unions and other forms of worker representation and participation, the rights and duties of the employer and employees and their representatives, how to deal with matters concerning conflicts and disputes, and also cooperation with unions, as well as how the organisation will relate to other related institutions, such as employer organisations or associations (Bendix 2010). Traditionally, the focus of labour relations management was primarily on the collective, conflicting and formal dimensions of employment relations (Nel 2012). However, the individual dimension is also covered in aspects such as the rights of the employee regarding fair treatment, accommodation, annual leave, certificate of service, family responsibility leave, freedom of association, maternity leave, notice of termination of employment, payment on termination of employment, prescribed days off, remuneration due, safe working conditions, sick leave and the right to strikeIndustrial actions (Grogan 2009).

Issues related to communication, information sharing and the handling of grievances, discipline and dismissal are also typically included in labour relations management. Human resource management usually covers the whole spectrum of functions from recruitment, selection and appointment to those functions aimed at fully utilising and developing the potential of all employees, as well as those aimed at caring for, rewarding and conserving the workforce (Nel 2012).

As such, the employment relationship and its management form the factor that binds the two fields of study, which traditionally were mainly dealt with separately in literature and management science, namely labour relations management and human resource management. Cowling and James (1994) put it as follows: "Too often personnel [human resource] management and the industrial [labour] relations are treated as two entirely different subjects" (p. 1). Through the above discussion, it is safe to identify employment relations as the component of the EOR where the rights and regulations of the relationship are identified, applied and controlled. This is therefore further discussed as employment regulations.

3.2 Employment Regulations

The desire on the part of both management and employees to exert control is an inherent characteristict of the employment relationship (Cappelli 1999). This power struggle to control directs the type of employment relationship that forms, as well as the balance of obligations and expectations negotiated, and sustained, in the psychological contract (Rubery et al. 2002). The employment relationship, as stated previously, is not in isolation from the society in which it is formed. Therefore, the approach to labour relations, associated with the wider society in which the employment relationship is formed, regulates and guides the features of this relationship (Reynolds et al. 1991).

Through the identification of four basic forms of labour relations, being *market individualism*, *liberal collectivism*, *bargained corporatism* and *state corporatism*, Salamon (1998, p. 271) accentuates the influence of collective bargaining (through the power position of trade unions) and the dominant political ideology of a country in the formation of the above-mentioned power balance (or imbalance) in the employment relationship. In the case of *market individualism*, very low collective bargaining in a liberalist-dominated political ideology exists (Fox 1971). With *liberal collectivism*, a strong autonomous power position of trade unions exists in a liberalist dominant political ideology (Finnemore and Van Rensburg 2000). *Bargained corporatism* refers to a high collective bargaining in a corporatist political ideology, while *state corporatism* consists of a weak and regulated power position of trade unions in a corporatist political ideology (Poole 1986). The influence of regulations, through legislation, on the employment relationship is one of the main characteristics that Salamon (1998) identifies in the above-mentioned approaches to labour relations.

Table 3.1 Labour legislation and organisational regulations associated with the types of labour relations approaches

Labour relations approach	Labour legislation	Organisational regulations
Market individualism	• Strong property rights by law • Passive labour law • Common law	• Tacit and verbal employer-orientated rules • Harsh sanctions for misconduct of employee (corporal punishment and dismissal) • Minimum disciplinary and other procedures • No or limited dispute resolution procedure
Liberal collectivism	• Modest legal framework • Non-government intervention • Individual agreements between employer and employee • Common law	• Negotiated rules between individual employee and employer • Organisationally based procedures and policies • Sanctions and actions scrutinised by unions • Non-regulated labour action used by unions as part of dispute resolution
Bargained corporatism	• Active state interference in consultation/negotiation with other parties • Strong labour legislation • Strict application of labour regulations • Collective bargaining structures	• Policies and procedures must be within clear regulations of labour legislation • Collective bargaining rights for organisational procedures and policies • Clearly regulated dispute resolution procedures, governed by labour law
State corporatism	• Labour suppressed by strict labour legislation • Minimum bargaining structures	• Labour law identifies organisational procedures and policies • Minimum collective bargaining rights • State-governed dispute resolution procedures

Source Bendix (2010), Finnemore and Van Rensburg (2000), Salamon (1998)

Table 3.1 identifies the forms of regulations that can be associated with the different approaches to labour relations, as well as the types of regulations within the employment relationship that can be associated with the approaches. This table furthermore amplifies the influence of the labour relations approach on the rules and regulations within the employment relationship. Venter and Levy (2011, p. 242) refer to the above-mentioned labour legislation and organisational regulations as implicit regulations, in the case of the former, and explicit regulations, in the case of the latter. To properly achieve the research objectives of this chapter, regulations will be addressed by focusing on the characteristics of implicit and explicit regulations as experienced in South Africa, taking the South African approach to labour relations into account.

3.3 The South African Approach to Labour Relations

Finnemore (1996, p. 7) emphasises the importance of acknowledging the history of South African labour relations to understand the current approach to it, as well as the associated labour regulations. Therefore, a brief overview of the history of the South African labour relations is necessary to acquire insight into the ideologies and motives sustaining the current approach to labour relations in South Africa, before it is discussed, in association with its influence on the regulation of the employment relationship.

Various sources (Bendix 2010; Finnemore and Van Rensburg 2000; Pons and Deale 1998; Venter and Levy 2011) identify three main labour relations eras in South African history. These eras can be summarised as the eras of *paternalism and exploitation* (colonialism), *separatism and adverserialism* (Apartheid), and *codetermination and cooperation*.

These eras, as summarised with highlights in Fig. 3.1, commenced with the ***era of paternalism and exploitation***, which refers to the time of slavery, by both European and African slavers (Chinweizu 1987; Dugdale et al. 2001), colonialism and the misuse of land ownership in the southern African employment relationships (Anstey 2002). In this era, where the employee depended on the owners of land and capital for life resources, the power in the relationship was one-sided, with the employer setting the rules and regulations of employment (Adejumobi 2000). Very little legislation regulated employment relationships, except common law, which mainly protected property rights of employers (Skaperdas 1992). Therefore, the employment relationship was mainly governed by the rules set by the employer, with limited legal regulations, giving the employer unlimited power in the relationship (Venter and Levy 2011).

Since industrialisation had already started developing in this era, due to more mining activities and manufacturing companies being found, the practice of using common law in labour relations started to become inadequate, as Grogan (2009, p. 4) states, "the common law lagged behind conditions in modern commerce and industry". Therefore, the first South African (at that stage the Cape Colony) labour legislation was also introduced during this era. However, it was basic and employer-orientated, being the Masters and Servants Act of 1841 (Webb and Webb 1960). Owing to industrialisation and mining activities in the country, many European, Australian and American tradesmen immigrated to South Africa to bring in specialised skills into these sectors (Pons and Deale 1998). The influence of these immigrants led to the introduction and implementation of the idea of

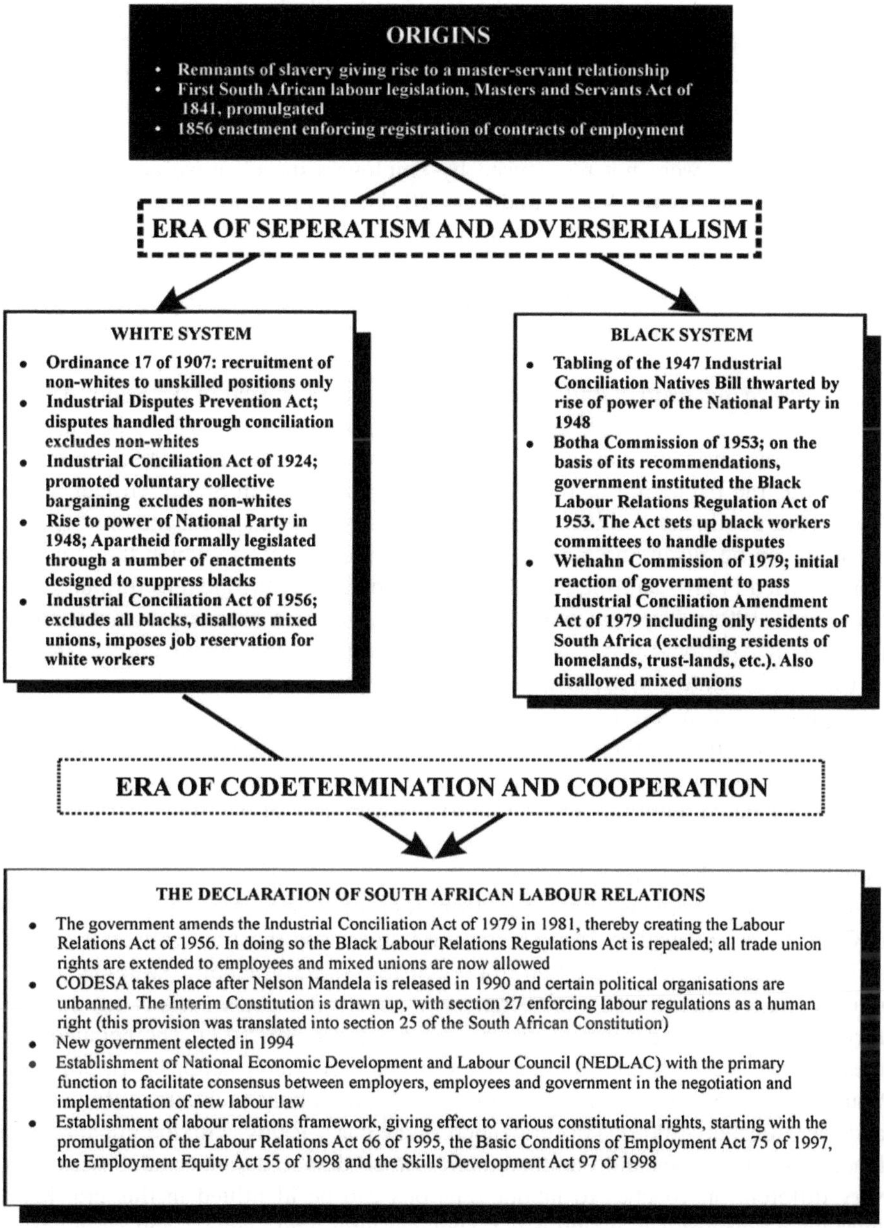

Fig. 3.1 Development of South African labour relations (adapted from Venter and Levy 2011, p. 35)

collective bargaining through labour unionism in South African labour relations (Cunningham and Slabbert 1990; Finnemore and Van Rensburg 2000).

An identifiable dualism in the labour market started to appear, with unionised (mainly white) tradesmen being one part of the labour force, and unskilled (mainly black) general workers being associated with the other part of the labour force (Lawrence 2000). While the former group started to balance the power struggle in the employment relationship, due to union activities, the latter group still experienced vigorous exploitation in the workplace (Tustin and Geldenhuys 2000). At the end of the nineteenth century, black employees started organising labour unions, but they were not recognised by employers in collective bargaining like their white counterparts (Venter and Levy 2011). This era continued until the early twentieth century (around 1907; Pons and Deale 1998) and can be closely associated with the approaches of *market individualism* (in the early stages of the era) and *liberal collectivism* (in the later stages of the era, when more union activities were realised, but little labour legislation regulated the relationship) to labour relations.

The ***era of separatism and adverserialism*** was introduced in the South African labour relations through the publishing of Ordinance 17 of 1907, wherein non-whites were restricted to unskilled positions (Van Jaarsveld et al. 1999). This ordinance was the beginning of formalised racial separatism in South African labour law, which continued and increased until the early 1980s, as indicated in Fig. 3.1. This era can be closely associated with the political stages in which the Union of South Africa (1910) and the Republic of South Africa (1961) were formed (Pons and Deale 1998). This era was dominated by racial separatism by law (forming part of Apartheid), as well as emergent political and labour unrest (Bendix 2010). While white employees received more rights and power in the relationship, through union recognition and job reservation, black employees were governed by strict laws that limited their rights and power, especially through the restrictions of black union activities (Pons and Deale 1998; Venter and Levy 2011). This period is also associated with the growing political awareness of the South African black population, through the establishment of various political parties and the later banning of most of these organisations.

Labour organisations, with the Congress of South African Trade Unions (COSATU, established in 1985) being the biggest and most active labour organisation in South Africa, played an important role in the freedom "struggle", when unions aligned themselves increasingly with political organisations to fill the void formed by the banned political parties (Venter and Levy 2011). The behaviour of these labour organisations included well-organised mass actions, crippling the South African economy, which led to even stricter labour regulations (Finnemore and Van Rensburg 2000). This era ended in the early 1990s, with the unbanning of black political parties and the movement to total democracy in South Africa. Two very different approaches to labour relations can be identified in this era, being *bargained corporatism*, which was associated with white labour, and *state corporatism*, which black labour experienced.

The current ***era of codetermination and cooperation*** can be contributed to the process of achieving equal rights in the South African constitution and the resultant legislation. In this process, all unfairly discriminating legislation has been systematically dissolved, starting with the negotiations during the drafting of the new constitution. Labour relations legislation also experienced transformation, through negotiations in Nedlac, formed in 1995, among the various parties in South African labour relations. The promulgation of various new labour acts, as previously mentioned and discussed below, introduced a *bargained corporatist* approach to labour relations for all South Africans for the first time.

The current approach to labour relations entails a clear legislative framework, applicable to all South African employees (with limited exclusions based on inherent requirements of positions). These regulations identify the framework wherein individual employment regulations can be negotiated. Labour regulations can therefore be divided into implicit regulations, associated with the regulations of the current national labour relations approach, and explicit regulations, being specific regulations within the individual employment relationship, both of which influence the experience of employment relations regulations (Slabbert and Swanepoel 2001).

Implicit regulations, as rights of the parties to a work relationship, are not expressly stated in a contract or implied by the past conduct or behaviour of the parties. Apart from being contained in the Constitution, these regulations are most commonly found in the labour statutes. In a country with a bargained corporatism approach to labour relations, these regulations are part of the social and legal contract in the labour relationship, since the constitution and labour legislation are negotiated by the various stakeholders (Salamon 1998). The implicit regulations, as indicated in Table 3.2, have various purposes, applications and interpretations, but in total they govern the parameters within which the employment contract and explicit regulations can be negotiated (Grogan 2009). The employment contract may not be less favourable than these regulations for both parties. As previously mentioned, since 1995 the implicit regulations have been transformed due to new and changing labour legislation. This change had to be incorporated in the employment relationship, influencing the employee–employer obligations and expectations therein.

Table 3.2 Changing employment regulations and its influence on an organisation's explicit labour regulations

Changing South African employment regulations		
Old implicit regulations	New implicit regulations	Adapted explicit regulations
Labour Relations Act 28 of 1956	Labour Relations Act 66 of 1995	Disciplinary and grievance procedure, recognition agreement, performance appraisal policy
Basic Conditions of Employment Act 3 of 1983	Basic Conditions of Employment Act 75 of 1997	Employment contract (e.g. working hours and leave), remuneration policy
–	New Employment Equity Act 55 of 1998	Employment equity policy (including psychometric testing, performance appraisal and affirmative action policies)
Manpower Training Act 56 of 1981	Skills Development Act 97 of 1998	Skills development and/or training policy

Explicit regulations are the rights and rules primarily set down in the employment contract, and the related organisational policies, procedures and codes. These regulations are closely associated with the specific employment relationship and are based on the negotiated employee and employer obligations (Rousseau 2001). However, in practice, these explicit regulations flow mainly from organisational initiatives and generally accepted labour relations practice based on standard policies, procedures and codes as associated with the current implicit regulations (Bendix 2010). In South African labour practice, these regulations are mainly used to control conflict (Venter and Levy 2011). Tustin and Geldenhuys (2000, pp. 107–112) identify three sources of labour-related conflict in an EOR, namely being distributive, structural and human relations causes.

- **Distributive causes of conflict**
  This form of conflict includes conflict that arises in formulation or operation of economic or substantive contracts or agreements. They are based on the problem of allocation or distribution of rewards for the performance of work. The initial stimulus for this cause of conflict may not necessarily emerge from the organisation, but rather from the market situation beyond the organisation's boundaries. In such situations, ***performance appraisal policies***, for individual reward adaptation, and collective bargaining, as governed in ***recognition agreements***, between recognised trade unions and the organisation, for annual organisational wage increases, are used. Owing to the changing socio-economic system in South Africa, ***employment equity*** and ***skills development policies*** are used explicitly by organisations to regulate the expectations created by the implicit regulations, being the Employment Equity Act (55 of 1998) and the Skills Development Act (97 of 1998). In certain cases, organisations also implement an ***affirmative action policy***, as part of or in addition to an employment equity policy.
- **Structural causes for conflict**
  These causes are the bases of the sort of problems that emerge from the interactions brought about by the formal structure of the organisation and are usually the result of a failure to structure the organisation properly, especially in situations of change. This area of conflict is not always as manifest as the issues of distributive conflict, and therefore does not receive that much interest, but it can lead to serious levels of conflict if not attended to.
  Processes that can minimise this form of conflict mainly involve role clarity through a clear job description in the ***employment contract***, as well as clear descriptions of employee and employer expectations and obligations contained therein. This can be extended to sanctions associated with non-compliance with the aforementioned expectations and obligations in a ***disciplinary code*** and procedure. The rules associated with the disciplinary code, which must be in compliance with implicit regulations, confirm the employee's obligations. If the employer's obligations are not met by the organisation, the employee can lodge a grievance through the ***grievance procedure***.

- **Human relations causes for conflict**
  Human relations causes underlie the sort of problems that emerge from the more informal, interpersonal level of interaction. This is an important area of conflict, since ultimately all conflict is manifested at the human relations level, whether its cause lies at the distributive or at the structural level. The sources of interpersonal conflict are personal differences, information deficiency, role incompatibility and environmental stress (Luthans 1998). In the main, the source of these conflicts is not directly associated with employee rights, as is the case with the former-mentioned sources of conflict, but rather with individual or group interests. In the cases where this conflict arises, the use of the ***grievance procedure*** for grievances of interest is the most common and recommended formal practice. Informal practices, including an open-door policy by top management, will improve the settlement of such conflict.
  Employers also apply regulations to advance a specific organisational culture, in addition to the aforementioned explicit regulations that are used to control conflict in the workplace. These forms of explicit regulations must be relevant in that there must be a fair reason for the practice and are mainly associated with the organisation's vision, mission and goals (Bendix 2010). Such forms of explicit regulations can include dress codes, customer service procedures and other rules that are not generally accepted (Venter and Levy 2011). These forms of rules can be incorporated in the ***disciplinary code*** (Salamon 1998).

The above-mentioned procedures, policies and codes to control conflict in the EOR are (directly or indirectly) prescribed and controlled by implicit regulations, through South African labour legislation. Should it not be implemented in EORs by organisations (where necessary), or applied unfairly, employees may make use of labour dispute resolution mechanisms, as regulated by labour legislation (the Labour Relations Act 66 of 1995, as amended). In certain cases, the employee, or groups of employees, acts outside the prescribed parameters of the labour legislation. These very radical and unprotected actions can include sabotage, assault illegal industrial actions (e.g. unprotected strikes) or wilful damage of individual and organisation property. Actions, both in accordance with the parameters set by labour legislation and unprotected or illegal actions, can lead to financial and relational consequences for the employer (Tustin and Geldenhuys 2000). Therefore, successful application of explicit regulations, controlling conflict in the EOR, is essential in an organisation.

The influence of the changing implicit regulations on the explicit regulations of the EOR is summarised in Table 3.2, where the interrelationship between these types can be identified. It can also be stated that the explicit regulations influence the implicit regulations, owing to new precedents being established through generally accepted practices (Bendix 2010; Nel 2012; Venter and Levy 2011).

As stated previously, the experience of the employment regulations by employees has a very important impact on the experience of the psychological contract, as well as the EOR in total.

3.4 Experience of Employment Regulations

A model developed and tested by Linde et al. (2008) explains the process of experiencing employment regulations. This model was based on the assumption that for an employee to experience employment regulations very positively, which will lead to commitment and high levels of compliance, the following should be realised:

- there should be clarity about the contents and reasons for the regulations; and
- the employee must trust the reason for and the application of the regulations.

For an employee to have **clarity** about the regulations in the specific employment relationship, the policies, procedures and codes associated with them must be *available* to the employee, the employee must *ascertain* the *contents* of the regulations and the employee must *understand* the contents.

3.4.1 Availability

The policies, procedures and codes that regulate the employment relationship can be made available to the employee in various forms, including:

- as part of, or attached to, the employment contract;
- in a general and known point in the workplace (e.g. the human resource department);
- as part of a collective agreement (e.g. a recognition agreement between the employer and a representing trade union);
- electronic (e.g. the organisation's website or through e-mails);
- verbally; and
- tacit.

The less formal the rules of the employment relations are, the higher the risk of the rule being invalid. Therefore, verbal or tacit conveying of employment regulations is not contributing successfully to clarity of the regulations (Bendix 2010; Grogan 2009; Venter and Levy 2011). Only when the regulations are reasonably and understandably available to the employee can the following step to clarity be realised.

3.4.2 Ascertainment

The employee needs to know the contents of the available regulations. This process is regularly applied through the induction programme upon employment. In certain cases, employees use their own initiative to make sure of the contents of the regulations, or use trade union representation for this purpose. However, the employer cannot apply a rule if the employee does not know the rule, therefore the employer cannot expect the employee to know the contents of employment regulations on own initiatives (Grogan 2009).

3.4.3 Understanding

Other than ascertaining regulations, the Code of Good Practice (Schedule 8 of the Labour Relations Act 66 of 1995) does not compel the employee to understand employment regulations for disciplinary procedures to be fair. But, if the employee understands the contents of the employment regulations, and the reasons for them, codetermination through role interpretation can be achieved (Salamon 1998; Tustin and Geldenhuys 2000). It is not possible for the employee to understand the employment regulations if ascertainment thereof was not realised, which cannot happen if they are not available.

The processes of obtaining clarity include changing employment regulations, implying that the process of availability, ascertainment and understanding should apply where the procedures, policies and codes of the employment relationship change (Venter and Levy 2011).

The second prerequisite for codetermination through role internalisation is **trust**. Similar to the understanding of employment regulations, the Labour Relations Act (66 of 1995) ("the Act") does not require trust in a rule or regulation to make it valid. The Act does stipulate that "...the employer's rule must create certainty and consistency in the application of discipline" (Schedule 8, s(3)(1)). Furthermore, an employee must accept a rule as fair to trust it (Bendix 2010; Coser 1971; Venter and Levy 2011). However related, this concept of trust in the procedures must not be directly associated with trust processes between people, as discussed by writers including Nooteboom and Six (2003) and Small (2004).

3.4.4 Acceptance

According to Nel (2012), a foreign labour relations policy, procedure, process or system can easily be adopted through consultation with the relevant representative parties. After consultation has been concluded and everything is clear, the policy, procedure, process or system is more easily accepted. Usually, after acceptance the organisation will implement such policies, procedures, processes or system and forward them to the staff of the organisation (Slabbert and Swanepoel 2001). This general practise underlies the principle of role internalisation, the importance of communication and the development of joint gaols. If the employee accepts the rule or regulation as fair, the employee will comply readily with the rule and accept the use of perceived fair discipline when the rule is not upheld. When the employee does not accept the rule or regulation, codetermination is limited, since the employee's actions are not interacting with the organisation's reasons for the rule (Charon 1995; Tustin and Geldenhuys 2000).

3.4.5 Trust in Application and Consistency

The misuse of employment regulation procedures by the employer limits the trust of employees in these procedures (Bendix 2010). Grogan (2009, p. 112) refers to situations where fair procedures for dismissal were used for unfair purposes, e.g. the use of a disciplinary hearing to dismiss an employee, for the reason of employing a relative in that position, or where retrenchments are carried out to dismiss employees who are union representatives, rather than for operational considerations. Such actions can collectively limit trust in the procedure associated with the regulation (Bendix 2010; Nel 2012; Tustin and Geldenhuys 2000; Venter and Levy 2011). The same principle applies to inconsistent application of a rule or regulation, either between employees, or to different actions of the same employee.

Figure 3.2 summarises the concept of clarity and trust in the experience of employment regulations by personnel, in the form of an integrated model. In this model, the constructs, *clarity* and *trust* correlate, with a medium effect (Jooste 2005; Linde et al. 2008). This implies that the trust in the management of employment regulations increases where these regulations are very clear to the employees. Furthermore, the above-mentioned writers identified a strong correlation between the subconstructs of *clarity*, associated with the types of employment regulations. In other words, the availability, ascertainment and understanding of

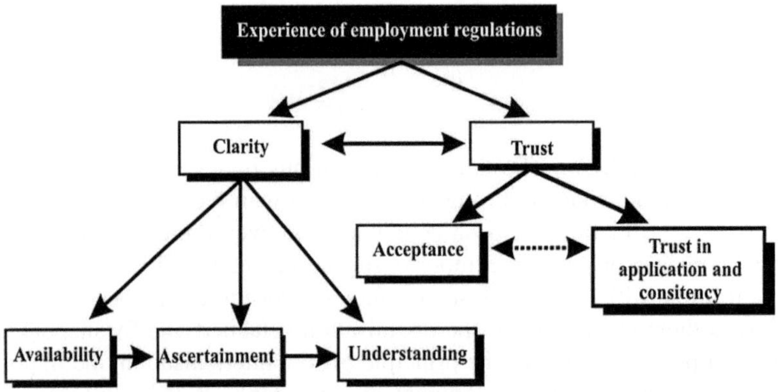

Fig. 3.2 Integrated model for testing the experience of employment regulations (*Source* Linde et al. 2008)

a type of regulation—e.g. disciplinary procedure—are experienced similar and therefore the clarity of that regulation is clustered.

Managing the employment relationship is a necessary process to establish a clear relationship that can also develop trust between the employee and employer. It is also a necessity to keep the employment relationship intact. A stable employment relationship will not guarantee a balanced and fulfilled psychological contract, but will contribute to a clear expectation and obligation process. This will enhance employee wellness and might limit conflict within the workplace. The next chapter will investigate the cost of work wellness from an individual, as well as collective level.

References

Adejumobi SA (2000) Politics and government. In: Falola FT (ed) African volume 2: African cultures and societies before 1885. Carolina Academic Press, Durham, pp 149–160

Anstey S (2002) Taking simplicity seriously? Natural resources and governance in northern Mozambique. Paper presented at the meeting of the International Union for the Conservation of Nature and Natural Resources—Southern Africa Sustainable Use Specialist Group, Paarl, South Africa

Bendix S (2010) Industrial relations in South Africa, 7th edn. Juta, Lansdowne

Cappelli P (1999) The new deal at work. Harvard Business School Press, Boston

Charon JM (1995) Symbolic interactionism: an introduction, an interpretation, an integration, 5th edn. Prentice-Hall, Englewoods Cliffs

Chinweizu I (1987) The West and the rest of us: white predators, black slavers and the African elite. Pero Press, Lagos

Coser LA (1971) Masters of sociological thought: ideas in historical and social context. Harcourt Brace Jovanovich, New York

Cowling A, James P (1994) The essence of personnel management and industrial relations. Prentice-Hall, London

Craig AWJ (1975) The industrial relations system. In: Barret B, Rhodes E, Beishon Collier J (eds) Industrial relations and the wider society. MacMillan, London, pp 8–20

Cunningham PW, Slabbert JA (1990) The historic development of South African industrial relations. In: Slabbert JA, Prinsloo JJ, Backer W (eds) Managing industrial relations in South Africa. Digma, Pretoria, pp 14–43

Dugdale A, Fueser JJ, Celso de Castro Alves A (2001) Yale, slavery and abolition. Amistad Committee, New Haven

Dunlop JT (1958) Industrial relations systems. Southern Illinois University Press, Carbondale

Finnemore M (1996) Introduction to labour relations in South Africa, 5th edn. Butterworths, Durban

Finnemore M (1999) Introduction to labour relations in South Africa, 7th edn. Butterworths, Durban

Finnemore M, Van Rensburg R (2000) Contemporary labour relations. Butterworths, Durban

Fox A (1971) Ideologies of management and collectivities. In: Barret B, Rhodes E, Beishon Collier J (eds) Industrial relations and the wider society. MacMillan, London, pp 169–261

Grogan J (2009) Workplace law, 9th edn. Juta, Kenwyn

Jooste FF (2005) The experience of the employee-organisation relationship by personnel in a South African mining organisation. Unpublished master's thesis, North-West University, Potchefstroom

Lawrence A (2000) Codetermination in post-apartheid South Africa? Politikon: S Afr J Polit Stud 27:117

Linde B, Schalk R, Linde HM (2008) Clarity and trust: the experience of workplace regulations by employees. S Afr J Labour Relat 32(2):86–103

Lumley R (1974) A modified rules approach to workplace industrial relations. Ind Relat J 10:49

Luthans F (1998) Organizational behavior, 8th edn. McGraw-Hill, Boston

Nel PS (2012) South African employment relations: theory and practice, 7th edn. Van Schaik, Pretoria

Nooteboom B, Six F (eds) (2003) The trust process in organizations: empirical studies of the determinants and the process of trust development. Edward Elgar, Northampton

Pons A, Deale P (1998) Labour relations handbook: a practical guide on effective industrial relations policies, procedures and practices for South African managers. Juta, Kenwyn

Poole M (1986) Industrial relations: origins and patterns of national diversity. Routledge & Kegan Paul, London

Reynolds LG, Masters SH, Moser CH (1991) Labour economics and labour relations. Prentice-Hall, New Jersey

Rousseau DM (2001) Schema, promise and mutuality: the building blocks of the psychological contract. J Occup Organ Psychol 74:511–541

Rubery J, Marchington M, Coopke FL, Vincent S (2002) Changing organizational forms and the employment relationship. J Manage Stud 39:645–672

Salamon M (1998) Industrial relations: theory and practice, 3rd edn. Prentice Hall, Hertfordshire

Shore LM, Tetrick LE, Taylor S, Shapiro JA-MC, Liden R, Parks JM, Morrison EW, Porter LW, Robinson S, Roehling MV, Rousseau DM, Schalk R, Tsui A, Van Dyne L (2004) The Employee-organization relationship: a timely concept in a period of transition. In: Martocchio JJ (ed) Research in personnel and human resources management, vol 23. Elsevier, Oxford, pp 291–370

Skaperdas S (1992) Cooperation, conflict and power in the absence of property rights. Am Econ Rev 82:720–739

Slabbert JA, Swanepoel BJ (2001) Introduction to employment relations management. Butterworths, Durban

Small AR (2004) Trust relationships: an exposition of three propositions. Unpublished master's thesis, University of Saskatchewan, Saskatoon

Labour Relations Act, no 66 of 1995. Government Printer, Pretoria, South Africa

Basic Conditions of Employment Act, no 75 of 1997. Government Printer, Pretoria, South Africa

Tustin C, Geldenhuys D (2000) Labour relations: the psychology of conflict and negotiation. Oxford University Press, Cape Town

Van Jaarsveld SR, Van Eck BPS, Kruger C (1999) Kompendium van Suid-Afrikaanse arbeidsreg, 3e uitgawe (Compendium of South African labour law, 3rd edn). Butterworths, Durban

Venter R, Levy A (eds) (2011) Labour relations in South Africa, 4th edn. Oxford, Cape Town

Webb JE, Webb B (1960) Industrial democracy. Longmans Green & Co, London

Wood SJ, Wagner A, Armstrong EGA, Goodman JFB, Davis JE (1975) The "industrial relation system" concept as a basis of theory in industrial relations. Br J Ind Relat 13:295

Chapter 4
The Economic Impact of Wellness

4.1 The Cost of Wellness

Work wellness can be differentiated between employee and relational wellness. Employee wellness research, where the individual experience has been studied, combines job satisfaction, job insecurity and the state of the psychological contract as important components thereof (Albrecht 2010; Rothmann et al. 2005). Work relational wellness refers to the collective relationship within the workplace context, which includes co-employee relations with employment and labour relations. Previously the psychological contract and the employment relationship were discussed as part of the EOR. In this chapter, both the individual and relational work wellness cost are investigated. First, the management and impact of the individual work wellness will be discussed, through focus on the state of the psychological contract job insecurity, job satisfaction and general health of employees. Thereafter, the management and cost of relational work wellness will be focussed on, with specific emphasis on industrial action, as a component of relational work wellness.

4.2 Individual Work Wellness and Its Cost

Figure 1.1 indicated the micro- and macroinfluences on the employment relationship. These influences have a direct impact on the employee's wellness, which will have an impact on the behaviour of the individual and cost to the organisation. The experience of breach and violation of a psychological contract have been confirmed as predictor for work wellness (Linde and Schalk 2008).

Chapter Aim The aim of this chapter was to identify the forms of wellness, associated with the workplace, and to establish the cost thereof.

B. Linde, *The Value of Wellness in the Workplace*, SpringerBriefs in Economics,
DOI 10.1007/978-981-287-402-3_4

4.2.1 The Psychological Contract and Wellness

Levinson et al. (1962) see the psychological contract as an exchange relationship between employer and employee in which each party has expectations about mutual obligations. The definitions that enjoy current prominence tend to emphasise the importance of the subjective understanding and experience of the individual employee (McLean Parks et al. 1998). According to Rousseau (1995), the psychological contract includes individual beliefs, shaped by the organisation, regarding terms of an exchange agreement between individuals and their organisation. Furthermore, the psychological contract is a mental model or schema comprising beliefs about the exchange relationship between employee and employer, and elements thereof can include beliefs about role responsibilities, job security and an employer's integrity (Pugh et al. 2003).

Certain authors make a distinction between contract breach and contract violation (see Morrison and Robinson 1997). A breach refers to the cognitive perception that the organisation has failed to uphold one or more aspects of the psychological contract (Hellgren 2003). A breach of the psychological contract is therefore based on the individual's perceptions of what an organisation has promised and how well the organisation has fulfilled such promises (Robinson and Morrison 2002).

A violation of the psychological contract refers to emotional and affective reactions such as those that can arise when the individual feels that the organisation failed to properly uphold its end of the psychological contract (Morrison and Robinson 1997). The effects of a psychological contract, and specifically its violation, can carry over to one's relationship with a new employer (Rousseau 1995, 2001). Empirical evidence on the formation of initial trust in new organisational relationships has shown that past experiences are an important determinant of an individual's intention to trust another party (McKnight et al. 1998).

Other empirical studies (Freese and Schalk 1996; Schalk et al. 1998, 2001; Schalk and Freese 2000) measuring the psychological contract include employer and employee obligations, violations of specific employer obligations, features of the relationship with the organisation (transactional–relational), affective commitment and intention to leave the organisation. Van der Vaart et al. (2013) also confirmed the relationship between the state of the psychological contract and the intention of employees to leave.

4.2.2 Job Satisfaction

Job satisfaction can be defined as an attitudinal state reflecting all the affective feelings that a person has about their job (Spector 1997). Locke (1976) refers to employee job satisfaction as a pleasurable emotional state resulting from the valuation of his/her work. It is an aggregate variable reflecting satisfaction towards facets of a job including growth, pay, co-workers and supervisors that contribute towards general satisfaction in varying degrees (Smith 1992). Furthermore, job satisfaction can be grouped into two dimensions, including intrinsic and extrinsic job satisfaction. Measuring these levels could correlate the levels of job insecurity with job satisfaction (De Witte 1999). Job satisfaction, especially job dissatisfaction, has a direct influence on employee well-being, and the work-related stress directly influencing it (Buessing 1999).

4.2.3 Job Insecurity

Sverke and Hellgren (2002) compiled a definition of job insecurity, which reads as follows:

Job insecurity has been defined as individual's "expectations about continuity in a job situation" (Davy et al. 1997, p. 323), "overall concern about the future existence of the job" (Rosenblatt and Ruvio 1996, p. 587), "perception of a potential threat to continuity in his or her current job" (Heany et al. 1994, p. 1431), and "Powerlessness to maintain desired continuity in a threatened job situation" (Greenhalgh and Rosenblatt 1984, p. 438). (p. 26)

Job insecurity, as a construct of employee wellness, can be experienced at a personal level (subjective) or attributed externally (objective; Ferrie 2001). Job insecurity includes both the possibility of becoming unemployed (cognitive assessment) and the emotional experience of the possible threatening situation (emotional reaction towards it). Despite the different ways of looking at and defining job insecurity, and the influence of the objective situation on the employees in South Africa, the subjective approach is predominant in the research of areas of work psychology and behavioural sciences. Therefore, the influence of subjective characteristics is deemed important as a stressor on employees in South Africa. Various researches (Dallender and Nolan 2002; Healy and McKay 1999; McLeod 1997) identified that job dissatisfaction is highly correlated to job insecurity, and the experience of physical and psychological ill health.

Employees exposed to organisational transformation experience job insecurity in the lead-up to the changes, and increased job demands after reorganisation, which have been shown, as mentioned, to have a negative impact on physical and mental health (Ferrie et al. 1995; Roskies et al. 1993). Role stressors, including ambiguities, conflict of interest and increased workloads may all contribute towards a lowered morale in the case of post-transformation workers (Swanson and Power 2001).

4.3 Relational Work Wellness and Its Cost

Employment relations deal essentially with people who, because of their mutual involvement in the working environment, have been placed in a specific relationship with one another (Bendix 2010). The employment relationship is not only the focus of labour relations on the specific employee–employer relationship; it also forms the basis of human resource management (Slabbert and Swanepoel 2001). Therefore, employment relations are a combination of labour relations management and human resource management, within the individual relationship between the employee and employer (Shore et al. 2004).

Labour relations management deals with decision-making and behaviour regarding aspects such as trade unions and other forms of worker representation and participation, the rights and duties of the employer and employees and their representatives, how to deal with matters concerning conflicts and disputes, and also co-operation with unions, as well as how the organisation will relate to other organisations, such as employer organisations or associations (Bendix 2010). Traditionally, the focus of labour relations management was primarily on the collective, conflicting and formal dimensions of employment relations (Nel 2012). However, the individual dimension is also covered in aspects such as the rights of the employee regarding fair treatment, accommodation, annual leave, certificate of service, family responsibility leave, freedom of association, maternity leave, notice of termination of employment, payment on termination of employment, prescribed days off, remuneration due, safe working conditions, sick leave and the right to strike (Grogan 2009).

Issues related to communication, information sharing and the handling of grievances, discipline and dismissal are also typically included in labour relations management. Human resource management usually covers the whole spectrum of functions from recruitment, selection and appointment to those functions aimed at fully utilising and developing the potential of all employees, as well as those aimed at caring for, rewarding and conserving the workforce (Nel 2012).

Various authors (Bendix 2010; Nel 2012; Tustin and Geldenhuys 2000; Venter and Levy 2011) acknowledge the importance of clarity and certainty of policies and procedures regulating employment relations, as well as the experience of their application. With the changing labour relations, due to the sociopolitical changes in South Africa and the transformation of the labour relations approach, employees will experience a difference in their employment relations. Testing the clarity of employment policies and the employee's trust in the new employment relations could identify levels of satisfaction and security in this relationship (Bendix 2010; Nel 2012; Tustin and Geldenhuys 2000; Venter and Levy 2011).

Diligence in the application of labour relations regulations in the workplace seems to be the most proactive process of minimising costs to the organisation. This process can establish a balanced and clear psychological contract that can be kept intact. Figure 3.4 also confirms that the management of labour regulations should include a process of clarity and trust. Even though this process is part of management practice, the results of perceived breach and violation of the psychological contract by employees can result in individual work wellness decreasing, as well as employees acting through collective bargaining processes to react on these breach experiences. Industrial actions are the most prominent act of collective dispute resolution processes.

4.4 Link Between Industrial Actions and Wellness

As in most industrialised countries, South African trade unions are facing a decline in their political and industrial influence in general (Fairbrother and Yates 2003). This does not, as such, influence the levels of industrial actions, but even seems to increase it. For only the second time in history, South Africa has lost over 10 million work days due to strikes in 2014. Schüssler (2014) indicates that the loss of man-hours increased significantly in South Africa in the past years, as shown in Fig. 4.1.

Generally, this has raised questions concerning the impact of trade union activities on the wages and working conditions of employees, as well as the reaction of trade unions. South Africa experienced prominent changes in the union landscape the past decade, where independent non-affiliated trade unions received growing popularity and union federation-associated trade unions experience a decline. This lead to new trade unions, of which some are associated with strong militancy and proneness for industrial actions, to surface in the South African labour relations landscape (Schüssler 2014). Of course, such level of industrial action has a cost, which is not only limited to economic and financial implications on the employer, but also on the wellness of employees. It is difficult to clearly indicate the cost of industrial action, since a lot of variables should be taken in account. Loss of man-hours has been perceived as a good guideline to the implication of the cost to company by the loss of production, as well as a loss of income. Other important contextual impacts on the link between industrial action and wellness include the time and length of the action, as well as the type of action that is applied.

Three recent South African case studies of industrial actions follow to investigate the link of it with individual and relational work wellness. The first case

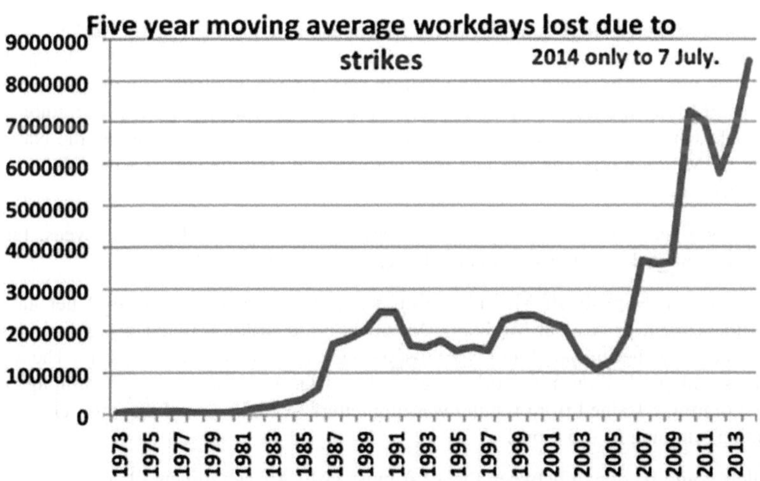

Fig. 4.1 Number of strike days lost five-year moving average (*Source* Schüssler 2014)

study, Marikana massacre, focuses on the individual and normative (group/trade union) impact of the strike on wellness. The second case study, Western Cape Farm workers' Strike, has a stronger focus on the communal impact of the strike, while the third case study, Platinum Mine Strikes of 2014, has a more South African economic impact of strikes on wellness.

4.4.1 The Marikana Massacre

One of the most violent reactions of South African Police Services (SAPS) took place as a result of an unprotected strike by platinum miners in 2012. The following article by South African History Online (2014) gives a clear picture of this event:

> On 16 August 2012, the South African Police Service opened fire on a crowd of striking mineworkers at Marikana, some 100 km northwest of Johannesburg in the North West Province. The fateful event left 34 mineworkers dead, 78 wounded and more than 250 people were arrested. The protesting mineworkers were demanding a wage increase at the Lonmin platinum mine. The event was the biggest incident of police brutality since the advent of democracy and it revived memories of the brutality suffered under Apartheid security police.
>
> Addressing a press conference, South African Police Service (SAPS) authorities claimed its officers had been under attack by a group of mineworkers armed with dangerous weapons, including machetes, spears and clubs when they opened fire with automatic weapons into the crowd a few meters away. Among those killed was Bongani Nqongophele, Janaveke Raphael, Van Wyk Sagalala, security guard Matlhomola Mabelane, Andries Ntshenyeho, Telang Mohai, Thabile Mpumza, Stelega Gadlela, Thabiso Thelejane, Thabiso Mosebetsane, Jackson Lehupa and many others. The official number of people killed was confirmed to be 34 by National Police Commissioner General Riah Phiyega, while 78 were injured and 259 arrested. The confirmation came after Police Minister Nathi Mthethwa told Talk Radio 702 that more than 30 people were killed and scores were injured.
>
> The unrest at the Lonmin mine began on 10 August, as more than 3,000 workers walked off the job over pay in what management called an illegal strike. The build-up to the massacre was marked by reports of intimidation and assault incidents among the different factions of mineworkers. Two police officers and two security guards counted among the 10 people who were killed as violence escalated between two rival unions, the National Union of Mineworkers (NUM) and the more radical Association of Mineworkers and Construction Union (AMCU).
>
> Striking workers infiltrated the production areas, assaulting on-duty employees, fatally wounding one and torching six motor vehicles at the plant.
>
> On 15 August, Minister of Mineral Resources, Susan Shabangu expressed her anxiety about the violent protests at Marikana. Meanwhile the striking mineworkers had chosen a hill as their gathering point and were discussing a truce with police officers. These discussions collapsed when mineworkers refused to disarm. Subsequently, the mining company, Lonmin, refrained from issuing warning letters to striking workers in order to avoid 'harming' ongoing negotiations.
>
> Parallels could be drawn between the 12 August 1946 African mineworkers' strike which was led by John Beaver (JB) Marks, leader of the African Mine Workers' Union (AMWU) and the 2012 mineworkers strike, led by Joseph Mathunjwa president of the Association

of Mineworkers and Construction Union. The 1946 strike was initiated by the Communist Party of South Africa (CPSA), which was active in distributing pamphlets and other material related to the strike. About 60,000 miners went on strike. The strike was forcibly suppressed by Government. According to 1946 official figures, nine workers were killed and 1,248 injured. Fifty-one persons, mainly Communists, were later charged in connection with the strike. They included three Indians, Dr Yusuf Dadoo, J.N. Singh and M.J. Vania. Police also arrested members of the District Committee of the Communist Party in Johannesburg. They were subsequently convicted and given sentences ranging from R30 (or three months in prison) to R100 (or six months' imprisonment).

The Marikana massacre prompted wide criticism, some calling it "the ANC's Sharpeville" while others claimed Marikana should be a catalyst for change. According to Terry Bell, Marikana was a watershed, a turning point that is likely to have a profound and long-term impact on South Africa's social and political environment. "But, unlike other watersheds over the past 53 years, it may provide the basis for political diversification rather than uniting disparate opponents of a single authority," he added. President Jacob Zuma cut short his attendance of the 32nd Southern African Development Community (SADC) Summit in Maputo, Mozambique, in order to visit the site of the incident. Announcing the government aims to appoint a commission of inquiry to probe the killings, Zuma said: "We have to uncover the truth about what happened here. In this regard I've decided to institute a commission of inquiry. The inquiry will enable us to get to the real cause of the incident." President Zuma appointed retired Judge Ian Farlam as Chairman of the Marikana Commission of Inquiry. His announcement came amid memorial services for the deceased held in the Eastern Cape, North West and Johannesburg.

While the commission is ongoing the allegations that have stemmed from it have caused concern over the police's version of the event. There have accusations of collusion between police, politicians and business to ensure the strike would be unsuccessful. The truth of these allegations will only come out after the commission has released its final report.

Various wellness impacts can be identified from this event, of which the ***loss of lives*** are the most obvious. The deaths associated with the Marikana massacre led to a total of 44 fatalities, of which ten people were killed in the weeks before the massacre. These ten deaths were related to the unprotected strike that the employees participated in, of which eight were employees and two were police and security personnel. The loss of income to 44 families not only had a financial impact to the community, but also an emotional stress.

The ***loss of income*** was not only due to the deaths of the strikers and security and police personnel, but also due to the strike action itself. In South Africa, the principle of "no work, no pay" applies to strikes. This strike was also an unprotected strike, implying that the striking employees could be disciplined by participating in it. In this case study, the actual strike was only from 10 August 2012 until 16 August 2012, except the aftermath in which the strike subsequently continued.

Thus, the ***loss of production*** should have been limited, if only loss of man-hours was taken in account. However, the impact of the intensity and type of the industrial action have also influenced the trust of investors in the mining company that was hit by the unprotected strike. An employer in South Africa has the right of recourse to lockout when an unprotected strike realise. This implies that employees that are willing and able to work do not have access to the workplace, with the same "no work, no pay" principle applying to them.

This can also be linked to the principle of solidarity, where the striking employees prohibited working employees to go to their work, by having picket lines and intimidating them. This has a huge impact on ***distrust of employee organisations***, especially the non-striking employees. With the mentioned case study, the industrial action was mainly due to a loss of trust in the recognised trade union and it lead to the formation of a new union that quickly became a majority union.

The tendency to resolve labour disputes through illegal and unprotected strikes took momentum, after the Marikana massacre, and two months later in 2012, a violent and intensive industrial action started in the Western Cape province.

4.4.2 Western Cape Farm workers Strike

After Marikana, the next industrial action case study to investigate the link thereof with wellness, was found in a very different sector and province. Only eleven days after Marikana, a group of mainly female farm workers stopped working, as part of an unprotected strike. This action quickly spread through the province's agricultural sector. The following article of Davis (2013) was published one year after this industrial action and summarises it:

> Western Cape farm strikes: one year on, still a political football (by Rebecca Davis, 28 October 2013 in the Daily Maverick).
>
> This week marks the one year anniversary of the strikes by Western Cape farm workers which left three workers dead, saw R160 million claimed for in insurance, and resulted in a 52 % increase in the minimum wage for the sector. There are commemorations planned in De Doorns and elsewhere, but there's also the potential for tension between farmers and farm worker unions who say that working conditions are still less than ideal.
>
> What BAWUSA (the Bawsi Agricultural Union of South Africa) is calling the "Farm worker Revolt" began almost exactly a year ago in the fruit farming communities of the Western Cape. Farm workers wanted to see the sectoral minimum wage brought up from its paltry R69 a day to R150. They didn't end up with R150, but from March, when Labour Minister, Mildred Oliphant, posted the new sectoral wage determination, a day's work as a farm labourer is not supposed to earn you less than R105 a day.
>
> When the 52 % increase was announced, there was much dramatic talk of the inevitable job losses that would follow, as farmers would not be able to afford the additional wage burden. In reality, this hasn't happened. Business Day reported in August that the quarterly labour force survey showed that agricultural employment only dropped by 3.5 % between March and August despite the addition of R2 billion to the wage bill. Agricultural economist, Nick Vink, was quoted as saying that despite the hype around the minimum wage increases, "there does not seem to have been a lot of concern about the R105. I think everyone agreed that R69 was too low."
>
> But that's not to say that everything's peachy now. BAWUSA and its controversial leader, Nosey Pieterse, claimed in a recent press release that farmers were exacting revenge for the pay hike through measures which include increasing the rent paid by farm workers, and increasing the tariffs paid by farm workers for electricity. "We note with concern that female workers, especially seasonal workers, bears [sic] the brunt of this retaliation of farmers," BAWUSA stated. (The union did not respond to the Daily Maverick's request for specifics on these allegations.)

In March, participants in a protest outside Parliament in Cape Town made various separate claims about the ongoing struggles of farm workers. A memorandum delivered by the 'Farm Worker Coalition' alleged that workers were being tricked or forced to sign forms indicating that they would be happy to receive less than R105 per day. It was also claimed that some farmers would only employ coloured workers, and not black workers, after the strikes.

Farmers, unsurprisingly, deny these charges. "Labour relations are actually fine," one told the Daily Maverick, speaking on condition of anonymity.

But there's no denying that some tensions have persisted beyond the official ending of the farm workers' strikes in January this year. The complicated saga of Flippie Engelbrecht, the teenage son of a Robertson farm worker allegedly beaten so badly by a farmer that he ended up losing both his hands, appeared to shed an ugly light on the ongoing mistreatment of workers by farmers - and indeed it still may. But when the farmer in question, Rietvallei's Johnny Burger, committed suicide in September, questions began to be asked about the medical timeline of the story, and about the woman behind it, Carina Papenfus.

Papenfus and her 'Freedom Trust' have gone on to produce a number of other farm workers who have allegedly also been victims of farmer brutality. Papenfus has repeatedly shown herself to be willing to adjust facts to support her cause, however. For instance, the Freedom Trust has been carrying out lobbying around the killing of a Worcester farm worker, Ricardo Zempie, who was shot in the head from behind, allegedly by the farmer in whose employ Zempie was.

The Freedom Trust has sought to present the murder as if it was connected to the sector labour unrest. In an August press release the Trust explained it as follows: "During the farm strikes, Ricardo Zempie, a farm worker, was shot in the back and killed by the farmer in whose employ he was." But newspaper reports suggest that Zempie was killed almost nine months before the farm strikes began, in February 2012, allegedly while attempting to steal cables.

This is, of course, irrelevant to the central point of the story: it is undeniably shocking that it appears nobody has yet been charged with Zempie's murder. Although farmer Johan van der Merwe was taken into custody the day after the shooting, he was apparently released almost immediately. An investigation to see whether he should be criminally charged is still ongoing.

There also appears to have been silence from the police on the matter of the investigation of three farm workers killed during the last year's strikes - Michael Daniels, Letsekang Tokhwane and Bongile Ndleni - even though IPID (Independent Police Investigative Directorate) spokesman Moses Dlamini told the Daily Maverick that the body has a maximum of 90 days to complete their inquiries. When we asked Dlamini in August what progress had been made in investigating the death of Michael Daniels, he replied that one policeman would be charged, and that the matter had been postponed till the end of September for a regional court date.

BAWUSA says that it has planned memorial services for the three men who died during the strikes, to take place over the weekend of November 2 and 3. In addition to the memorials, the union will lead "celebrations" in "De Doorns and in all other areas that participated in the strike".

De Doorns, the impoverished epicentre of the strike, shows signs of becoming something of a Western Cape political football in the run-up to the 2014 elections. In October, Minister of Social Development, Bathabile Dlamini, and Trade and Industry Minister, Rob Davies, visited De Doorns and delivered food parcels. The ANC denied charges that this amounted to vote-buying, saying that it was simply part of the government's outreach programme to poor communities.

Also in October, Labour Minister, Mildred Oliphant, visited another area hard-hit by the strikes – Citrusdal – to address farm workers at the Cederberg Academy and remind them

> to whom they owed the increased minimum wage. "If it weren't for the ANC there would be no sectoral determination," Oliphant reportedly said. "That is why the ANC does not govern the Western Cape, because some of you have decided not to vote."
>
> DA leader Helen Zille, meanwhile, has continued to suggest that the farm strikes were fomented by the ANC to destabilise the Western Cape. "Why… did Agriculture Minister Tina Joemat-Pettersson's department transfer R2-million to an organisation led by Nosey Pieterse, an ANC cadre, shortly before it fuelled the violent strike on Western Cape farms last year?" Zille wrote in her SA Today newsletter in mid-October.
>
> Zille seems to have been referring to reports in April that the other organisation Pieterse leads, the Black Association of the Wine and Spirits Industry (Bawsi), was receiving funds from the government. Bawsi, the Department of Agriculture told parliament, played a critical role in mobilising the striking workers "towards calmness and constructive engagement with the employers".
>
> We may have a clearer picture of the strike's catalysts when an independent research project is released. UCT's Centre for African Studies and the Surplus People's Project have been running the project, investigating the causes and leaders of the farm strikes, for much of the year. The report is scheduled to be completed in December.
>
> As the one-year anniversary approaches, BAWUSA alleges that tensions between farmers and farm workers are increasing. "Emotions are running high in the De Doorns area," read their most recent press release. "Farmers are being mobilized to prepare themselves and to go on the offensive." BAWUSA claims that farmers hope to derail the union's celebrations by organizing their own farm workers' march on 30 October. "It is a pity that our celebrations must now be strained but we have no plans to disappoint you," the union said. "We will be there, waiting for you. Battle ready."
>
> Farmers say these threats are nothing more than characteristic grandstanding and publicity-seeking from Nosey Pieterse. In communities still shaken by the violence of last year's unrest, many will be hoping they're right.

The Western Cape Farm Strikes are very different than the Marikana strike, where the farm workers' strikes showed a strong ***communal welfare motivation***. The strikes actually also included civil unrest, since many of the protesters partaking in the series of protests were not only farm workers, but included a large number of sympathisers and family members of the workers. The strikes also effectively exposed the low wages in this sector and the industrial actions played an important role in the prominent ***increase of minimum wages***.

The ***political connection*** between industrial action and labour unrest was also visible in this case study. The Western Cape province is the only one of nine South African provinces not in the power of the ruling African National Congress (ANC). Thus, various allegations of political influence were made between political parties.

4.4.3 The Platinum Mine Strike of 2014

On 23 January 2014, nearly 70,000 platinum workers in the Rustenburg area went on strike for five months. The strike affected all three of South Africa's major platinum producers and it ended on 24 June 2014. This unique level of labour unrest resulted from deadlocks in wage negotiations between the trade unions and related platinum mines. Other than the first case study—Marikana massacre—the strike was protected where the applicable procedures were followed before it. Thus, the employees were safeguarded not to be disciplined for partaking in it. The following news article of the South African Broadcasting Corporation (SABC News 2014) was published after the end of the strike:

Platinum strike still affecting economy

Tuesday 9 September 2014 17:10

The repercussions of the five-month-long platinum strike are still affecting the country's economy, the SA Reserve Bank (SARB) said. Real Gross Domestic Product (GDP) fell 0.6 % in the first quarter of the year and then rose in the second quarter by an annualised rate of 0.6 %, according to the bank's Quarterly Bulletin. The SARB said "This barely positive growth rate was extremely disappointing given the country's development needs, and was mainly brought about by the drawn-out industrial action in the platinum-mining subsector which started on 23 January 2014 and only came to an end five months later."

South Africa would have been considered to be in a recession had there been two consecutive quarters of negative growth. The bank said the platinum sector strike, which resulted in a sharp contraction in mining output in the first quarter, led to a "further but less drastic decline" in real mining production in the second quarter. The conditions extended to the electricity sector, where weakness in demand was amplified by a relatively mild winter and a higher real price of electricity.

"By contrast, the agricultural sector registered stronger growth in real output over the period, supported by a bumper maize crop." A decline in commerce sector activity and slower growth in the real value added by the financial services sector were offset by growth in the transport and general government services sectors in the second quarter. The SARB said growth in real final consumption expenditure by households decelerated further in the second quarter.

This was consistent with the deceleration in the real disposable income of the household sector as industrial action detracted from striking workers' earnings. Growth in the general government service sector's real final consumption expenditure accelerated slightly in the second quarter, partly because of the national and provincial elections in May.

The country's export performance in the second quarter was inhibited by strikes, logistical and energy constraints, a moderation in global demand, and a decline in some commodity prices. SARB said employment trends reflected the generally subdued growth in economic activity.

"Enterprise-surveyed employment in the formal non-agricultural sector rose somewhat over the most recently available four quarters to the first quarter of 2014, but all the job creation took place in the public sector," it said.

SARB said the number of work days lost to industrial action had escalated since the beginning of the year. "Average wage settlements increased moderately over the past year, although a number of high-profile settlements were in double-digit territory." It said fiscal policy continued to provide support to economic recovery.

"The public-sector borrowing requirement amounted to 4.6 % of gross domestic product in April/June 2014, slightly higher than a year earlier. Both general government and the non-financial public corporations continued to incur more expenditure than their current revenue as they aligned their infrastructure and other programmes with the targets set out in the National Development Plan. In the most recent quarter, however, general government raised its share of the borrowing requirement whereas public corporations decreased."

This strike did not only have a five-month impact of production losses, but it also took three months for the mines to return to normal production. This strike was the longest and most expensive in South African history and did not only influence the South African markets, since almost forty percentage of the world's platinum production was shut down as a result of the strike. Africa Leader (2014) reported that the "platinum mining companies, it is estimated, collectively lost between US$2 and 2.4 billion during the five month strike with the workers loosing close to US$1 billion in lost wages". The toll of the strike was substantial and directly influences the ***South African economic growth***.

The country's GDP did not increase, even though wage increases were part of the results of the strikes, since a huge ***loss of personal income*** was the result of a five-month "no work, no pay" industrial action. Schüssler (2014) confirms that the average wage increase will not subdue this effect of five months' loss of income and that many of the striking employees increased their debts in this period by making short term loans.

4.4.4 Proposed Link Between Industrial Action and Wellness

An individual's willingness to participate in industrial action is connected to the question of the individual's work wellness. The risk of losing an income in the period of industrial action should be well motivated. It is also confirmed by Kochan (1980) that individuals can share collective wellness of peers, once an individual is associated with a collective bargaining structure, such as trade unions. Thus, the individual's work wellness can lead to participation in collective bargaining structures, which can lead to industrial action. The association to collective bargaining structures, itself, can also influence the individual's wellness.

It is prominent that the cost of industrial action—protected or unprotected—is significant for both the individual that participate in it, as well as the employer, the community and the society. South Africa also experienced a socio-economic cost through the loss of investor trust in the company. This realises through the loss in revenue of the employer that directly reflects on growth—value-adding to the economy. The reputation that the employer, as well as the sector, earns for not being able to supply has a major trust impact. The length and intensity of many strikes damages the labour market's reputation and the investors can easily choose to move their trust to other more stable labour markets, which could increase job insecurity.

The financial benefits of wage increases due to industrial actions are not the only important results for employee organisations participating in it. Industrial action also has a sociopolitical impact of increasing a power structure. A settlement, even due to large personal losses of individual members, increases the image of solidarity and commitment of a trade union, which will have an impact on future negotiations. In South Africa, where the ruling political party has a commitment with the largest union federation, this show of solidarity of an independent trade union also has a strong political impact.

Table 4.1 Proposed links of wellness with industrial action

Individual wellness		Employment wellness	
Negative	Positive	Negative	Positive
• Loss of lives • Intimidation and violence • Loss of income/benefits • Job insecurity • Loss of skills (due to injury/trauma) • Retraining	• Wage increase	• Possible discipline • Distrust in relationship • Formalisation of contract • Increased production goals	• Impact on future negotiations • Better employment conditions • Job opportunities for replacement workers
Normative wellness		**Social wellness**	
Negative	Positive	Negative	Positive
• Violent trade union competition at workplace level • Solidarity focus, rather than individual focus by trade union • Intimidation and violence • Impact on collective negotiation structures (independent union without national influence)	• Sense of belonging • Unified trade union members	• Impact on economic growth • Impact on labour legislation • Precedent of illegal industrial actions • Impoverished communities on short term	• Low–minimum wages exposed • Community growth on long term

Heaney et al. (2006) confirm that individual wellness does influence the employee's willingness to participate in industrial action. This confirms that individual wellness plays a role in the individual's decision-making process to start acting in protected or unprotected industrial action to voice unhappiness against the employer, even to the cost of loss income. Sverke et al. (2004) indicates that a higher level of job insecurity does not decrease the willingness of an individual to participate in industrial action, but can rather increase collective bargaining activities that can also lead to industrial actions. This same relation exists with decreased job satisfaction levels. In general, lower levels of work wellness of employees will increase collective bargaining activities and participation in industrial actions. This relationship is also applicable to the wellness of employees who participates in industrial action. The loss of income and the impact of such actions on the trust relationship in the workplace influence the job insecurity and satisfaction levels. With struggling markets, a weak currency and cheaper imports, it is likely to mean that the South African workforce might experience more insecurities, which will directly influence individual's wellness levels.

The cost of industrial action has clear influences on the individual, the organisation, communities and also on the wider society. Table 4.1 proposes the link between industrial actions and wellness. This proposition differentiates between individual and collective wellness, as well as formal and informal influences. Both negative and positive wellness aspects are also proposed.

In the conclusion chapter, the economic value of wellness in the workplace will be summarised, after which a framework of the influence of the EOR on work wellness, including the economic value thereof, will be proposed.

References

Africa Leader (2014). Platinum mine workers in South Africa return to work, 25 June 2014. Retrieved 26 June 2014 from http://www.africaleader.com/index.php/sid/223255797/

Albrecht SL (ed) (2010) Handbook of employee engagement: perspectives, issues, research and practice. Edward Elgar Publishing, Northampton

Bendix S (2010) Industrial relations in South Africa, 5th edn. Juta, Lansdowne

Buessing A (1999) Can control at work and social support moderate psychological consequences of job insecurity? Results from a quasi-experimental study in the steel industry. J Work Organ Psychol 8(2):219–242

Dallender J, Nolan P (2002) Mental health work observed: a comparison of the perceptions psychiatrists and mental health nurses. J Psychiatr Ment Health Nurs 9(1):131–137

Davis R (2013) Western Cape farm strikes: one year on, still a political football, 28 Oct 2013. In: The daily Maverick. Retrieved 17 Sept 2014 from http://www.dailymaverick.co.za/article/2013-10-28-western-cape-farm-strikes-one-year-on-still-a-political-football/#.VDPYHPmSxqU

Davy JA, Kinicky AJ, Sheck CL (1997) A test of job security's direct and mediated effects of survivor responses to layoffs. J Organ Behav 18:323–349

De Witte H (1999) Job insecurity and psychological well-being: review of the literature and exploration of some unresolved issues. Eur J Work Organ Psychol 8(2):155–177

Fairbrother P, Yates C (eds) (2003) Trade Unions in renewal: a comparative study. Continuum, London

Ferrie JE (2001) Is job insecurity harmful to health? J R Soc Med 94(22):71–76

Ferrie JE, Shipley M, Marmot MG, Stansfield S, Davey-Smith G (1995) Health effects of anticipation of change and non-employment longitudinal data from the Whitehall II study. Br Med J 311:1264–1269

Freese C, Schalk R (1996) Implications of psychological contracts for human resource management. Eur J Work Organ Psychol 5:501–509

Greenhalgh L, Rosenblatt Z (1984) Job insecurity: toward conceptual clarity. Acad Manage Rev 3:438–448

Grogan J (2009) Workplace law, 10th edn. Juta, Kenwyn

Healy C, McKay M (1999) Identifying sources of stress and job satisfaction in the nursing environment. Aust J Adv Nurs 17(3):30–35

Heany CA, Isreal BA, House JS (1994) Chronic job insecurity among automobile workers: effects on job satisfaction and health. Soc Sci Med 38:1431–1437

Heaney CA, Israel BA, Schurman SJ, Baker EA, House JS, Hugentobler M (2006) Industrial relations, worksite stress reduction, and employee well-being: a participatory action research investigation. J Organ Behav 14(5):495–510

Hellgren J (2003) The times they are a-changin': job uncertainty and the flexible labor market. Akademitryck, Edsbruk

Kochan TA (1980) Collective bargaining and industrial relations: from theory to policy and practice. Irwin, Homewood

Levinson H, Price CR, Munden KJ, Mandl HJ, Solley CM (1962) Men, management and mental health. Harvard University Press, Cambridge

Linde B, Schalk R (2008) The influence of pre-merger employment relations and individual characteristics on the psychological contract: a South African case study. S Afr J Psychol 38(2):305–320

Locke E (1976) The nature and consequences of job satisfaction. In: Dunnette MD (ed) Handbook of industrial and organizational psychology. Rand McNally College Publishing Co, Chicago, pp 297–349

McKnight DH, Cummings LL, Chervany NL (1998) Initial trust formation in new organizational relationships. Acad Manag Rev 23:473–491

McLean Parks J, Kidder DL, Gallagher DG (1998) Fitting square pegs into round holes: mapping the domain of contingent work arrangements onto the psychological contract. J Organ Behav 19:697–730

McLeod T (1997) Workstress among community psychiatric nurses. Br J Nurs 6:569–574

Morrison EW, Robinson SL (1997) When employees feel betrayed: a model of how psychological contract violation develops. Acad Manag Rev 22:226–256

Nel PS (2012) South African employment relations: theory and practice, 7th edn. Van Schaik Publishers, Pretoria

Pugh SD, Scarlicki DP, Passell BS (2003) After the fall: layoff victims' trust and cynicism in re-employment. J Occup Organ Psychol 76:201–213

Robinson SL, Morrison EW (2002) The development of psychological breach and violation: a longitudinal study. J Organ Behav 21:525–546

Rothmann S, Steyn LJ, Mostert K (2005) Job stress, sense of coherence and work wellness in an electricity supply organisation. SA J Bus Manag 36(1):55–63

Rosenblatt Z, Ruvio A (1996) A test of a multidimensional model of job insecurity: the case of Israeli teachers. J Organ Behav 17:587–605

Roskies E, Lewis-Guerin C, Fournier C (1993) Coping with job insecurity: how does personality make a difference? J Organ Behav 14:617–630

Rousseau DM (1995) Psychological contracts in organizations: understanding written and unwritten agreements. Sage, Thousand Oaks

Rousseau DM (2001) Schema, promise and mutuality: the building blocks of the psychological contract. J Occup Organ Psychol 74:511–541

SABC News (2014) Platinum strike still affecting economy, 9 Sept 2014. Retrieved 9 Sept 2014 from http://www.sabc.co.za/news/a/798e5400456906ab8741a7c7c599c9eb/Platinum-strike-still-affecting-economy

Schalk R, Campbell JW, Freese C (1998) Change and employee behaviour. Leadersh Organ Dev J 19:157–163

Schalk R, Freese C (2000) The impact of organizational changes on the psychological contract and attitudes towards work in four health care organizations. In: Isaksson K, Hogstedt C, Eriksson C, Theorell T (eds) Health effects of the new labour market. Kluwer, New York, pp 129–143

Schalk R, Heinen J, Freese C (2001) Do organizational changes impact the psychological contract and workplace attitudes? A study of a merger of two home care organizations in the Netherlands. In: De Jonge J, Vlerick P, Büssing A, Schaufeli WB (eds) Organizational psychology and health care at the start of a new millennium. Rainer Hampp Verlag, Munich, Germany

Schüssler M (2014) Strikes are also about inequality and reputation, 9 July 2014. Retrieved 21 July 2014 from http://www.moneyweb.co.za/moneyweb-soapbox/strikes-are-also-about-inequality-and-reputation

Shore LM, Tetrick LE, Taylor S, Shapiro JA-MC, Liden R, Parks JM, Morrison EW, Porter LW, Robinson S, Roehling MV, Rousseau DM, Schalk R, Tsui A, Van Dyne L (2004) The employee-organization relationship: a timely concept in a period of transition. In: Martocchio JJ (ed) Research in personnel and human resources management, vol 23. Elsevier, Oxford, pp 291–370

Slabbert JA, Swanepoel BJ (2001) Introduction to employment relations management. Butterworths, Durban

Smith PC (1992) In pursuit of happiness, why study general job satisfaction. In: Cranny CJ, Smith PC, Stone EF (eds) Job satisfaction: how people feel about their jobs and how it affects their performance. Lexington Books, New York

South African History Online (2014) Marikana Massacre, 16 Aug 2012. Retrieved 11 Aug 2014 from http://www.sahistory.org.za/article/marikana-massacre-16-August-2012

Spector PE (1997) Job satisfaction: application, assessment, causes, and consequences. Sage Publications, Thousand Oaks

Sverke M, Hellgren J (2002) The nature of job insecurity: understanding employment uncertainty on the brink of a new millennium. Appl Psychol: Int Rev 51(1):23–42

Sverke M, Hellgren J, Näswall K, Chirumbolo A, De Witte H, Goslinga S (eds) (2004) Job insecurity and union membership. Series: Travail & Société/Work & Society, vol 42. European Unions in the Wake of Flexible Production

Swanson V, Power K (2001) Employees' perceptions of organizational restructuring: the role of social support. Work Stress 15:161–178

Tustin C, Geldenhuys D (2000) Labour relations: the psychology of conflict and negotiation. Oxford University Press, Cape Town

Van der Vaart L, Linde B, Krugell M (2013) The state of the psychological contract and the intention to leave: the mediating role of the employee well-being. S Afr J Psychol 43(3):356–369

Venter R, Levy A (eds) (2011) Labour relations in South Africa, 3rd edn. Oxford University Press, Cape Town

Chapter 5
Conclusion

5.1 Conclusions

The role of this chapter is to draw conclusions and to provide deductions and viewpoints that arose from the arguments in the previous chapters. Before these conclusions are made, a summary of the contents of the previous chapters will be given, with practical and theoretical implications of the findings. Thereafter, a wellness model will be proposed, which is based on the practical and theoretical conclusions of the book. Recommendations will follow these overall conclusions.

In Chap. 2, the link between the psychological contract and wellness was established. There is a clear indication that an individual's general health is influenced when breach and violation of the psychological contract exists. This can be seen in the increase of job insecurity levels of such individuals (De Witte 1999). Job satisfaction levels also decrease as breach and violation of the psychological contract realises (Healy and McKay 1999). This influence on the individual's wellness associated with the workplace has an impact on the work relationship between the employer and employee (Hellgren 2003). Various studies (Hellgren 2003; Linde et al. 2008) concluded that such increase of job insecurity and decrease in job satisfaction has an impact on the cost to the company. Absenteeism was linked with such lower levels of work-related wellness, and presenteeism has also been linked with them. Furthermore, a breach and violation experience between the parties to the employment relationship can influence the trust relationship.

Chapter Aim This book focuses on the link between the employee–organisation relations (EOR)—the employment relationship and the psychological contract—and the economic value of wellness—individual and relational. This was approached by first discussing the psychological contract, including the impact thereof on individual wellness. Thereafter (Chap. 3), the employment relationship, as part of the EOR, was looked at from a South African context. Chapter 4 focused on the economic value of wellness in the workplace, where the individual and relational impacts were discussed.

B. Linde, *The Value of Wellness in the Workplace*, SpringerBriefs in Economics,
DOI 10.1007/978-981-287-402-3_5

The psychological contract is a very important component of the employee–organisation relationship (EOR). The psychological contract is mainly associated with individual experiences of wellness in the workplace. The psychological contract is the influence that changes an objective situation into a subjective experience. This implies that a fair and acceptable contract of employment can change into a subjective negative experience due to various external influences (Katz and Kahn 1978; Hellgren 2003). These influences can include characteristics of the individual, as well as those of the other party in the relationship. Normative influences through group association, such as union or employer organisation membership, are the influences that change the objective situation to such subjective experiences. This shows that fair employment agreements within acceptable labour relations approaches can be perceived as unfair due to individual and social influences. The social aspects that can influence the subjective experience include the changing labour relations of South Africa, as well as a transformed sociopolitical sphere.

South Africa is perceived as one of the most unequal societies, since this country is still struggling to cope with the legacy of apartheid. The South African Gini coefficient is one of the highest in the world. A major reason for this remains the difference in quality of skills development of black and white South Africans (Reddy 2000). South Africa has experienced high levels of sociopolitical change during the past few decades. The dismantling of Apartheid, as part of the previous government's official policy, mainly contributed to this change. The taking over of government from the former National Party by the current ruling African National Congress after the first democratic elections in 1994 emphasised this transformation. This newly elected government immediately started to replace and change separatist legislation with new laws within the provisions of the new Constitution of South Africa. Labour law, and the acts of Parliament associated with it, was one of the priorities of changing legislation. Since 1995, a series of changed and new pieces of labour-related legislation permanently changed the South African labour relations system into a social corporatist approach—where centralised negotiations and consultations are encouraged in the development of South African labour relations. The influence of the changing South African sociopolitical system was not limited to new government and legislation, but also affected all other social systems in the country, either directly or indirectly. The history of racial segregation figured very strongly in the past and still influences the current labour market as a whole.

After centuries of white minority rule, it cannot be expected that these inequities change in a short period of time, but it seems that it is not changing fast enough. This shows the increase of inequity from 1994 to a larger Gini coefficient in 2009 (Worldbank 2014). This has a huge impact on wellness on various spheres. The semi-skilled and unskilled labour remains frustrated in workplaces where huge remunerations are given to skilled employees while the semi-skilled and unskilled labourers are responsible for the biggest bulk of the production. The South African mining and agricultural sectors are good examples of this. This influences the membership of trade unions in South Africa as well as industrial action to address this inequity.

The alliance between the ruling ANC government and the largest trade union federation—COSATU—also increases the frustration of these labourers. They experience that their trade union leaders are too close to the political power of the ANC and big business to focus on the needs of their members. This makes the participation of independent new trade unions very desirable.

In the South African trade union history, where these employee organisations also had a role in the struggle against apartheid, it was important to focus on solidarity, rather than on individual needs. This is currently still a big role in union activities where it is expected that the collective objectives of trade unions are prioritised against individual representation and needs. To enforce this perception of solidarity, employees in South Africa experience intimidation of non-unionised employees or union members who do not want to participate in industrial action. This background and current situation puts stress on individuals, which again influences their work-related wellness. Such individuals cannot expect that their needs will be prioritised, and they must also participate in industrial actions, even if they do not agree with it. Furthermore, an individual may be in an employment agreement which is perceived as fair—an objective situation—but due to the normative influences (solidarity) they are forced to show dissatisfaction with this agreement—a subjective experience. These influences also made an impact on the normative experiences within the EOR. From a society with a history of separatism, a strong collectivism realised in the labour relations milieu.

It can be stated that the psychological contract experience can be influenced by the individual's work wellness, but also that work wellness of the individual can influence the psychological contract. Even with external influences on the psychological contract, the experience of breach and violation should not automatically end the employment relationship. The current cooperatist labour approach in South Africa allows the management of the employment relationship through corrective and progressive measures to keep the relationship intact, even where contract breach realises (Bendix 2010). This can be done through policies and procedures from the employer to address acts of the employee that can be perceived as contract breach. Such procedures include disciplinary guidelines, as well as poor work performance policies and even retrenchment procedures. The main purpose of disciplinary procedures is to correct the unacceptable behaviour of the employee. By this, the psychological contract breach by the employer can be managed. However, the employee can also experience breach, which can be handled through grievance procedures. Such procedures are supposed to allow grievances of rights and interest to be addressed in a way which is a safe forum for the employee to express himself without fear of victimisation or prejudice.

A grievance of right is an individual grievance associated with legitimate expectations of the employee that was not fulfilled by the employer. These grievances usually relate to contractual obligations such as salary, hours of work, leave entitlements and benefits. Should these grievances not be resolved within the workplace, the employee can then refer it to the dispute resolution mechanism applicable to his workplace. A grievance of interest is usually bargained collectively through trade unions, or staff associations, and employers on an organisational or sectoral level. An example of a grievance of interest may be annual cost of living adjustments. If these grievances are not resolved in the workplace, they are also referred to the dispute resolution mechanisms [Commission of Conciliation, Mediation and Arbitration (CCMA) and bargaining councils] referred to above. A dispute of right will be arbitrated through the labour dispute resolution mechanism, where a final award will be handed down. With a dispute of interest, the South African labour resolution mechanism cannot arbitrate it, but will allow the trade union to continue with a strike action that will be perceived as protected.

Unprotected strikes are associated with disputes that did not follow the correct dispute resolution procedures. Participants in these strikes can be disciplined and even dismissed for partaking in these types of strikes. Participants in protected strikes cannot be disciplined for participating in strike action, but replacement workers may be used in their positions. This explains the importance of solidarity with industrial action to limit the use of replacement workers, as they are intimidated and victimised when they present themselves to work at the employer.

South Africa has seen an increase of unprotected strikes in the past two years. This was highlighted with the Marikana massacre of 16 August 2012, where 36 employees participating in an unprotected strike were shot dead by the South African Police Services. After that incident, various unprotected strikes, with a major impact on production level, realised. The Western Cape farm workers strikes, only weeks after the Marikana massacre, was the most prominent of these unprotected strikes. This type of industrial action is marred with violence, destruction of employer and community property, intimidation and even police reaction that lead to fatalities. Industrial actions, especially unprotected strikes, influence various wellness aspects. On an individual level, it increases the possibility of job losses due to disciplinary actions against participants in unprotected strikes. It also limits the income of participants of unprotected strikes due to the principle of "no work, no pay". It was reported that many participants of these types of industrial actions went into microloans with high interest rates (Schüssler 2014). This increases the individual's stress levels, which have a big wellness impact.

Such activities also impact the wellness of groups, such as non-participating employees as they are exposed to intimidation and violence, as well as the possibilities of lockouts. The pressure to participate in a strike action can also force an employee to strike even when this individual did not plan to participate.

Industrial action, especially unprotected strikes, also places stress on the employment contract. Firstly, the increased conditions of employment, which was not on a scheduled negotiations period, could place the organisation in financial risk. Retrenchments are another option available to the employer to enable them to absorb this financial burden. The striking employees are usually the first to be included in such retrenchments, mainly due to the unskilled level of employment that they are associated with. Secondly, it can force the employer to apply the conditions of employment without flexibility, sometimes to the detriment of the employee. This might imply that the employment relationship changes from a relational agreement to a contractual agreement. A less sympathetic approach to the employee by the employer may be the result.

In Chap. 4, three case studies were used to illustrate the link between wellness and industrial action. It was clear that the wellness of communities associated with participating employees was negatively influenced by the action of said employees. This was due to high levels of intimidation and violence that these communities experienced, as well as a loss of income. Many striking employees in all three of the case studies left their workplaces to go to their rural homesteads, which also influenced small businesses of that area. It was also clear that the use of unprotected strikes as industrial action spread like wildfire through various sectors and became a powerful tool in the negotiation process.

5.2 Implications of the Research

This book identified the link between EOR's wellness in the workplace and the cost thereof. The practical contribution of this book is the holistic view on the challenges and opportunities that employees experience in a changing South African labour relations system, which also relates to international labour relations, from an individual and collective perspective. Specific components of these transforming employment relations were identified. The influence of a changing labour relationship was not only placed in context of the overall employment relationship, but also related to specific constructs, including the experience of regulations, job insecurity and satisfaction, and general health, as well as the cost thereof on individual and relational levels. From a practical point of view, this identifies a process where the overall experience of the changing employment relation by the employee can be dismantled into specific objective and subjective situations.

The ***practical*** implications were placed in a South African perspective. Practical examples, through three case studies, were identified and analysed through a work wellness approach. The influence of the experience of employment relationships and employee wellness was discussed. This leads to the proposal of an integrated model to illustrate this influence.

5.3 Proposed Integrated Work Wellness Model

In this model, the effects of an objective condition were linked to individual characteristics and social contexts. These aspects influenced the subjective experience of the employment relationship, being the psychological contract and experience of employment regulations. The employees' reactions to these conditions were experiences and influences that can be associated with their work wellness. Short-term work wellness reactions include job insecurity and work wellness, while general health can be associated with the long-term reactions. A strong relation was also found between the subjective experience of the psychological contract and work wellness. Clarity and trust in employment regulations were also identified as a moderating factor. It was also discussed that employees who trusted the employment regulations did not need high levels of clarity therein, while those with low trust did. Measuring clarity and trust in employment regulations, as a moderator of work wellness, can identify needs for employment regulations clarity, which can improve the employee's trust in it.

It seems that clarity and trust in employment regulations are not similar for all the types of regulations. This can be attributed to the management's focus on a certain type of regulation and the availability thereof. Furthermore, the levels of trust in a type of regulation also influence the employee's necessity to have clarity about it (e.g. an employee who trusts the management's application of the employment contract does not have a prominent need to examine the contents thereof). Identifying the types of employment regulations that are not trusted can also indicate the employee's need of more clarity on it. The theoretical implication of this conclusion is that three types of employment regulations can be grouped, related to the employment contract, conflict handling and performance control. It is also necessary to accommodate unrelated types of regulations, due to the diverse inherent requirements that can be part of an employment relationship. The experience of availability, ascertainment and understanding of a certain type of regulation can be expected to be very much similar, and clarity and trust in this type of regulation will be strongly related. The level of trust in a type of employment regulation does not seem to directly influence the level of trust in the others. Further investigation of the different moderating influences of the various types of employment regulations on work wellness can improve employment relations theory focussing on work wellness.

The overall conclusions are divided into two parts: practical, focussing on the South African context, and theoretical, focussing on the proposed integrated model (Fig. 5.1) and the influence of the results on employment relation theory.

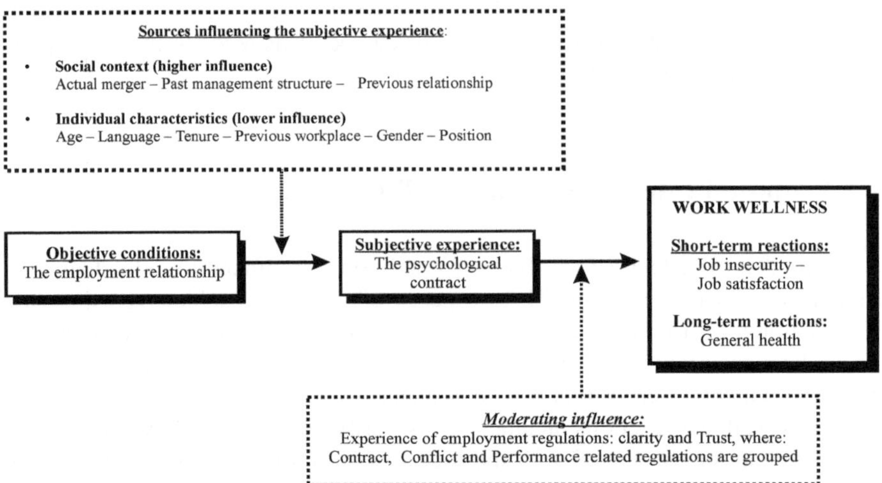

Fig. 5.1 An employment relationship and work wellness structural model

5.4 Practical Implications

Focus was placed on certain aspects of the psychological contract where breach and violation could be experienced. Possible reasons for these experiences of the psychological contract were identified. The results can therefore assist decision-makers in addressing certain experiences of violation, influencing work-related wellness, of the psychological contract. This can also give organisational change managers an indication of the importance of the psychological contract in the establishment of a new employment relationship.

The link between the EOR and work wellness indicates that the experience of the psychological contract has a direct link to work wellness on an individual level. It was also indicated that that this relationship can be managed by employment relations procedures. The relationship between the employer and employee does not need to end when either party experience a breach of contract. Corrective measures to keep the relationship in tact can be used through disciplinary and grievance procedures. However, clarity and trust in these structures are important for breach experiences to be moderated. Clarity in employment relations regulations consists of availability, ascertainment and understanding. The context of the employment relationship should be incorporated in the way in which these clarity components are best applicable to the unique relationship. Trust and clarity can be used effectively to moderate the individual wellness experiences at a workplace.

The individual relationship, however, can be influenced by collective aspects. These aspects, such as union activities, also influence the individual's experience of the EOR. Industrial action is a prominent reaction of the collective impact on the EOR. These actions can have a relational wellness impact on the workplace, as well as communities.

The message for (HR) managers is that they should avoid focusing on clarity of regulations when employees have no trust in fair application. Building a trust climate, on the other hand, will work positive because of the lower need for focusing on clarity, and the greater effects that can be reached to increase work wellness.

5.5 Theoretical Implications

Work wellness studies could differentiate between individual and relational experiences. The influences that change objective situations to subjective experiences should also include normative and social influences. The impact of independent variables, such as social context and normative influences, should not be underestimated in wellness studies.

The background of the psychological contract theory and the contents thereof were also revisited. The influence of individual characteristics on the psychological contract was compared with the social context in which the relationship was operating. It is clear that the influence of the social context has a bigger impact on the psychological contract, than the individual characteristics. This result motivates further studies focussing on the correlation between the experience of the psychological contract and the internal and external context in which it exists.

References

Bendix S (2010) Industrial relations in South Africa, 5th edn. Juta, Lansdowne

De Witte H (1999) Job insecurity and psychological well-being: review of the literature and exploration of some unresolved issues. Eur J Work Organ Psychol 8(2):155–177

Healy C, McKay M (1999) Identifying sources of stress and job satisfaction in the nursing environment. Aust J Adv Nurs 17(3):30–35

Hellgren J (2003) The times they are a-changin': job uncertainty and the flexible labor market. Akademitryck, Edsbruk

Katz D, Kahn RL (1978) The social psychology of organisations, 2nd edn. Wiley, New York

Linde B, Schalk R, Linde HM (2008) Clarity and trust: the experience of workplace regulations by employees. S Afr J Labour Relat 32(2):86

Reddy J (2000) Regional consortia, partnerships, mergers and implications for the transformation of the South African higher education system. S Afr J High Educ 14:87–97

Schüssler M (2014, July 9) Strikes are also about inequality and reputation. Retrieved 21 July 2014 from http://www.moneyweb.co.za/moneyweb-soapbox/strikes-are-also-about-inequality-and-reputation

Worldbank (2014) Data: the GINI index. Retrieved 25 Feb 2014 from http://data.worldbank.org/indicator/SI.POV.GINI

Index

B. Linde, *The Value of Wellness in the Workplace*, SpringerBriefs in Economics,
DOI 10.1007/978-981-287-402-3

FSC
www.fsc.org

MIX
Papier aus verantwortungsvollen Quellen
Paper from responsible sources
FSC® C105338

If you have any concerns about our products,
you can contact us on
ProductSafety@springernature.com

In case Publisher is established outside the EU,
the EU authorized representative is:
Springer Nature Customer Service Center GmbH
Europaplatz 3, 69115 Heidelberg, Germany

Printed by Libri Plureos GmbH
in Hamburg, Germany